W9-AXA-419

hunger

understanding the crisis

hunger

through games, dramas, & songs

Compiled and Edited by

Patricia Houck Sprinkle

John Knox Press
ATLANTA

Scripture quotations from the Revised Standard Version of the Holy Bible are copyright 1946, 1952, and © 1971, 173 by the Division of Christian Education, National Council of the Churches of Christ in the U.S.A. and used by permission.

Dedicated

to

All Who Are Hungry

and

All Who Labor to Feed them

Contents

Why & How

Games, Dramas, & Songs

why & how

why play games about
hunger?

Hunger is no game. While you read this paragraph, somewhere in the world an emaciated mother is watching helplessly while her infant gives one last weak cry and dies. A father is looking into the eyes of his children and wondering how to tell them he cannot feed them tonight no matter how hard he works today. An old man is just waking on a bare pavement and groaning for a swallow of clean water, a crust of dry bread. While you read this chapter hundreds of people will die from diseases directly caused by not having enough to eat. No, for the third of the world's people who daily go without adequate food, hunger is no game.

For most of us, however, hunger is unreal. When we read that thousands die daily from hunger, how can we picture that? But try this: imagine that you are at your dinner table when there is a knock at your door. When you answer, a gaunt man stands there, his cupped palms asking for food. Behind the man stands a potbellied child, behind the child a woman. Behind her you see a line of people that goes down your walk to the street, up the street out of sight, and then *around the world eight times!* That's one way of beginning to picture how many people are hungry in our world.

Most of us respond better to problems of hunger when those problems move from the realm of impersonal statistics into the realm of everyday life and familiar people. When we read that unemployment is on the upswing, we move on to the next news story; when our sister or brother shows up and says, "I've lost my job. How am I going to feed the children?" we become mobilized to seek solutions. Aware that "children are hungry in our world," we munch our French fries and vaguely wish there were something we could do; when our neighbor's kid shows up underfed, we reach for another plate. But how can we translate something as big as world hunger into personal terms?

Educators tell us we remember only about ten percent of what we hear, and about fifty percent of what we hear and see. But we remember approximately *ninety* percent of anything we *do*. This became real for me when I realized that the hunger facts I remembered best were those I had learned in hunger workshops through short, to-the-point games. By using songs, simulations, quizzes, role plays, and hunger meals, we begin actually to get inside hunger until

10

it becomes real for us. Then hungry people cease being, vaguely, "They" and become "We."

That's what this book is about. It contains some games to help explore Biblical bases for hunger action. (Does God have a point of view about hunger? What is it?) It contains other games to teach basic facts, to evaluate personal lifestyles, to simulate certain situations that cause hunger, and to experience what it feels like to be shunted off into hunger by circumstances beyond your control.

This book does not have many answers to the world hunger situation. What it does have is ways for well-fed people and groups to begin identifying with hungry people until we all care enough to start making our own answers.

You will notice as you read through the book that many of the games are similar. You will need to select carefully the ones best suited to your group or family and its situation. Many of the games are adaptable—as newer statistics become available, they can be fitted into the format of the game. Finally, you will find that most of the games are anonymous. That's because they have come from many sources. They were created by people who wanted to teach something about hunger in a short time. Very few were originated by professional game makers. Rather, they spread around the country via workshops until the original creator's name was lost, or the game had evolved beyond recognition. Some were even sent in as "original" from several parts of the country at once!

Perhaps that's the best part of these games. They were created by people like you and me. Chances are that as you get involved in playing them, you and your groups may come up with games you feel are better than the ones here. If you do, send them to me. If we get enough, we'll do a second anthology!

My prayer as this book is completed is that it may help stimulate some users to identify with and commit themselves to the world's hungry people because the hungry have ceased being faceless, meaningless masses and have become instead real mothers, fathers, brothers, sisters, and children of our own.

11

ways to use this book

SETTINGS

Most of the games in this book work best with families and small groups of up to twelve people. Many of them, however, can be adapted for larger groups. Some settings for which they are most appropriate are:

Have a weekly family hunger night at home, perhaps around your meal table (or later in the living room). Play one or two games from this book, then discuss together what you have learned. Create placemats for the family or decorate your refrigerator with some of the artwork suggested (see the cross-reference index at the end of this chapter for placemat and artwork suggestions). Create a family board game, such as Road to a Well-fed Village or Concentration. You might even consider how favorite family games could be adapted to teach facts about hunger—hunger Scrabble, for instance. Appendix I gives additional suggestions for families that want to become involved as a family in combatting hunger.

Have a special church night supper program on hunger. Set up your dining room so no more than eight persons are at a table, and let each table function as a small group. Select several games and perhaps a skit that you feel combine to give a well-rounded introduction to several facets of the hunger issue. If your first night is a success, keep track of the games you used and plan another night with different games later on. Chapter Eight, Food Experiences That Teach, contains several suggestions for meals that you might use as a part of the evening.

If children usually leave the dining room during your programs, ask those responsible for their programs to arrange for them to play Bible Picture Lotto, Picture Lotto, Concentration, or Starve the Man; perhaps older children might make individual games such as Road to a Well-fed Village to take home.

Make hunger a regular emphasis of church night suppers and other congregational meals (men of the church, etc.). Use placemat games and quizzes, sing hunger songs as part of your regular sing-along, and decorate your eating room with the Eye Chart, a Following Food Through the Bible Mural, or Parable Put-ups. Plan simpler but just as nourishing meals, and circulate new recipes.

Have a church school quarterly unit on hunger. A church school class might vote to suspend its regular quarterly study in favor of a hunger study, using some of these games to introduce each week's topic before delving deeper using any one of several excellent resources. (A few basic books and other additional resources are listed in Appendix II.) The leader or, preferably, planning committee

12

should study the games and select those best suited for your group. The quarter might culminate in a class decision to become involved in a specific mission project, political action, evaluation of the congregation's corporate life with regard for energy consumption, or other activity. You might also have a class party using one of the food events listed in Chapter Eight.

Use games as a part of workshops, retreats, and camps. Because these games take no more than one hour to play—and most of them take 15-20 minutes—they are ideal either to introduce various sections of hunger workshops or to make hunger one focus for weekend retreats or week-long camping experiences. Be sure, if they are incorporated into retreats or camps with another main theme, that sufficient time is allowed after the game for participants to discuss what they have learned and to suggest avenues for further study/action.

CHOOSING GAMES

The book is organized according to categories of games: Bible Games, Fact-finding Games, Lifestyle Evaluations, Songs, Longer Simulations, and Food Experiences That Teach. At the end of this chapter is an index which cross-references all games according to:

   a) type of game (quizzes and puzzles; analytical exercises, surveys, and inventories; simulations; skits and role plays; board games; artwork)
   b) time required for play;
   c) number of players necessary;
   d) suggested ages for players;
   e) special preparations, equipment or room arrangements necessary;
   f) special features: good for placemats, involves physical activity.

The book contains some games good for every age from five to ninety-five, for one to unlimited players, and for time-slots of three to sixty minutes. To use the games most effectively, therefore, consider the ages of your group, the size of your group, the time you have to play, and any other factors especially relevant to your own situation, then use the index to select those games that best meet your needs.

PREPARING TO PLAY

Each game is written up to indicate its purpose, any special materials and preparation needed before you begin to play, and procedure for play. *A leader should be sure to understand exactly how a game is to be played before introducing it to a group.* Sufficient quantities of materials needed should also be gathered ahead of time. This prevents valuable time being used on technique and material-gathering instead of on learning.

13

A CROSS-REFERENCE INDEX

GAMES LISTED BY TYPES

Categories:

Bible Games = BG
Fact-finding Games = FF
Lifestyle Evaluations = LE
Longer Simulation = LS

QUIZZES AND PUZZLES

Game	Category	Number	Under 5 minutes	5-15 minutes	15-30 minutes	30-60 minutes	Open	Open (1 or more)	2-8 (per team)	Large Group (15+)	Good for Placemats	Involves Physical Activity	Mixed Ages	Older Youth/Adults	Young Teens 11-14	Children 8-10	Children 5-7*	Prepare ahead!	Special equipment	Special room setup
God Feeds People	BG	1		•				•			•			•	•	•		•		
How Much Do You Know?	BG	2		•				•			•			•	•	•		•		
Meals Jesus Ate	BG	5		•				•			•		•					•		
He Said It!	BG	13	•					•			•			•	•	•		•		
Just Imagine It!	FF	17	•					•			•		•	•	•		•	•		
Starve the Man	FF	20					•		•						•	•				
World Hunger View Crossword	FF	25		•			•	•			•				•	•		•		

ANALYTICAL EXERCISES, SURVEYS AND INVENTORIES

Game	Category	Number	Under 5 minutes	5-15 minutes	15-30 minutes	30-60 minutes	Open	Open (1 or more)	2-8 (per team)	Large Group (15+)	Good for Placemats	Involves Physical Activity	Mixed Ages	Older Youth/Adults	Young Teens 11-14	Children 8-10	Children 5-7*	Prepare ahead!	Special equipment	Special room setup
Profiting from Prophets	BG	3			•				•					•	•	•				
The Debate	BG	7					•		•					•	•					
Letter from Beyond	BG	11			•				•					•	•	•				
What Do We Need to Know	FF	15		•				•						•	•	•				
Self-survey: Basic Factual and Value Choices	FF	18			•			•						•	•				•	
I Need, I Want, I Have . . .	LE	29			•				•		•			•	•	•		•		
Energy Consumption Inventory	LE	30		•					•					•	•			•		

SKITS AND ROLE PLAYS

Game	Category	Number	Under 5 minutes	5-15 minutes	15-30 minutes	30-60 minutes	Open	Open (1 or more)	2-8 (per team)	Large Group (15+)	Good for Placemats	Involves Physical Activity	Mixed Ages	Older Youth/Adults	Young Teens 11-14	Children 8-10	Children 5-7*	Prepare ahead!	Special equipment	Special room setup
Scripture Mini-skits	BG	10		•					•			•		•	•	•			•	•
Unto One of the Least	BG	14		•					•			•		•	•	•		•	•	•
How to Live on $100 a Year	FF	23		•					•			•		•	•			•	•	
What They See Is What They Get	LE	31		•	•				•			•		•	•	•		•	•	•

TO GAMES IN THIS BOOK

* Quizzes used with children 5-7 will probably need to be done orally rather than as written work.

** Can be used with tables of 6-8 persons, but 10-15 are better.

games, dramas, & songs

bible games

This section contains quizzes, mini-skits, and exercises designed to remind Christians that food is a spiritual as well as material question. These games can help lay a firm theological foundation for later data-gathering and hunger action.

A complete list of Biblical references found in these games appears in Appendix III.

Contents

Number	Game	Type	Time*
1	God Feeds People!	Quiz	5-10
2	How Much Do You Know?	Quiz	5-10
3	Profiting from Prophets	Scripture Analysis	20
4	Following Food Through the Bible	Artwork	30-45
5	Meals Jesus Ate	Quiz	5-8
6	Meals Jesus Ate — Placemat	Quiz	Open
7	The Debate	Scripture Analysis	Open
8	Parable Put-ups	Artwork	Open
9	Parable Placemats	Artwork	Open
10	Scripture Mini-skits	Drama	3-10
11	Letter from Beyond	Scripture Analysis	10-20
12	Bible Picture Lotto	Board Game	5-15
13	He Said It!	Quiz	5
14	Unto One of the Least of These	Drama	10-15

* In minutes (approximate)

19

1

Type: Quiz
Time: 5-10 minutes

God Feeds People!

(Reproduce one for each participant or read aloud for answers.)

Sometimes we think the Bible is concerned only about spiritual things. We forget how often eating and drinking are mentioned, and especially how often God takes care of material needs of the people. We are called to do the same. How many of these references can you get?

1. The first day God created light

   To give us warmth and heat.

   Five days later God made us

   And gave us _____ to eat. (Genesis 1:29)

2. For forty years the Hebrews lived

   Out on a desert trail.

   When they complained they had no food,

   God sent_____ and_____ . (Exodus 16:2-15)

3. Joshua's people

   Didn't have much money

   But the land God gave them

   Flowed with_____ and _____ . (Exodus 3:8)

4. _____ , hidden by the brook

   Was fed by birds unseen;

   He feared not prophets true to Baal,

   But fled a wicked queen. (1 Kings 17:1-6)

5. "Fasting to show off
   Disgusts me," God said.
   The fast he prefers is
   Sharing our _____ . (Isaiah 58:5-7)

6. Jesus said we're
   This old world's_____ .
   And if we're not tasty
   It's our own fault! (Matthew 5:13)

7. Jesus made picnics—
   Delectable dishes—
   With a schoolboy's lunch:
   Five _____ and two _____ . (Mark 6:30-44)

8. The men from _____
   Liked what he said
   But they didn't know Jesus
   Until he broke bread. (Luke 24:13-35)

9. Earthly life for Christians
   Is not all bread and jam,
   But we know we'll be invited
   To the _____ of the Lamb. (Revelation 19:9)

Answers: 1. plants 2. manna, quail 3. milk, honey 4. Elijah 5. bread 6. salt 7. loaves, fishes 8. Emmaus 9. supper

21

2

Type: Quiz
Time: 5-10 minutes

How Much Do You Know?

(Reproduce one for each participant or read aloud for answers.)

Through the prophets, God explicitly told us what he thinks about poverty and hunger in our midst. How much do you know about what God thinks? Take the following quiz, then look up the references to check your answers.

1. Because the poor are always going to be among us, we are to
   (a) realize that fact and let them work on their own problems
   (b) open our hands wide and treat them generously
   (c) let the government take care of them

   (see Deuteronomy 15:7-11)

2. God's price for wine and milk is
   (a) the going rate   (b) hard work   (c) nothing

   (see Isaiah 55:1)

3. God prefers
   (a) religious services   (b) shared bread   (c) frequent fasting

   (see Isaiah 58:5-7)

4. God thinks the following cause of death is worst
   (a) hunger   (b) war   (c) old age

   (see Lamentations 4:3)

5. God promises a day when
   (a) the plowman shall overtake the reaper and wine flow from hills
   (b) rich people shall be punished
   (c) those who worked hard shall have enough to eat

   (see Amos 9:13)

3

Type: Scripture Analysis
Time: 20 minutes

Profiting from Prophets

In the Old Testament God frequently expressed through the prophets opinions concerning the poor and hungry. The purpose of this exercise is to determine exactly what God's attitude toward the poor and needy seems to be, and to discuss how that might determine our own actions toward them.

MATERIALS NEEDED: Bibles, pencils, and paper for each participant or team.

PROCEDURE: Have each individual or team choose one of the following passages. Ask them to spend 5 minutes reading the passage and jotting down phrases that seem to express God's attitude toward food and/or hunger. As a group discuss such questions as:

What seems to be God's attitude toward food?

What seems to be God's attitude toward hunger?

What does God seem to expect his people to do for the poor?

What seems to be God's attitude toward those who neglect the hungry and poor?

What do these scriptures call on us to do?

If you have time, compare Isaiah 58:6-8 with Matthew 25:31-46.

SUGGESTED SCRIPTURES:

Deuteronomy 8:7-17	Description of the promised land
Deuteronomy 15:7-11	Laws concerning treatment of the poor in the land
Isaiah 55:1-3	"Ho, every one who thirsts . . . "
Isaiah 58:6-8	"Is not this the fast that I choose . . . "
Lamentations 4:4-9	Description of extreme hunger
Amos 9:13-15	Description of days to come
Micah 4:1-4	Description of days to come

4

Type: Artwork
Time: 30-45 minutes

Following Food Through the Bible

In many ways the story of the Bible is a story of food. Making a mural depicting some times when food was important in the Old and New Testaments can be an effective way to demonstrate just how often people's relationship to God closely paralleled their food situation.

MATERIALS NEEDED: Roll of plain shelf or butcher paper, Bibles, magic markers or crayons, tape, 3 x 5 cards. You will also need a long table or floor space to work on.

PROCEDURE: Depending on the size of the group, work individually or in teams.

Before the group assembles, the leader will want to write each reference (below) on a separate 3 x 5 card and number them in sequence. How many events you want to use will depend on your group and time.

Participants either draw or choose a card, look up the scripture reference, and illustrate that food event as s/he chooses *on the appropriate part of the mural paper*. When completed, the mural chronologically depicts important parts food played in the Biblical story.

You may want to display this mural around the walls of a fellowship hall, family room, sanctuary, or elsewhere where hunger is being studied.

FOOD EVENTS:

1. God creates food	Genesis 1:29
2. Food leads to first sin	Genesis 3:1-13
3. We are made to work for our food	Genesis 3:17-19
4. Food offered as a sacrifice to God	Genesis 4:1-8
5. Jacob uses food to usurp Esau's birthright (leads to founding of Israel)	Genesis 25:29-34
6. Hunger sends Israelites to Egypt	Genesis 41:53 – 42:7

7. Promise of food encourages Israelites to follow Moses	Exodus 3:7-8
8. A meal symbolizes God's salvation	Exodus 12:1-17
9. Food becomes a source of complaint and a proof of God's love	Exodus 16
10. Hunger sends Elimelech and Naomi to Moab, where their son marries Ruth	Ruth 1:1-5
11. In a barley field Ruth and Boaz become betrothed; thus David and Jesus get a foreign ancestress	Ruth 3, 4:18-22
12. Food again leads to sin; God uses this to establish Samuel as priest	1 Samuel 2:12-17, 3:1-11
13. God feeds a prophet	1 Kings 17:2-6
14. Food promised to the poor	Isaiah 55:1-3
15. Food: blessing and curse of God	Hosea 2:1-13
16. God's kingdom = Bread, not bullets	Micah 4:1-4
17. Satan tries to tempt Jesus initially through hunger	Matthew 4:1-4
18. Jesus' first miracle: feeding guests	John 2:1-10
19. Jesus feeds minds, hearts, and bodies	Mark 6:30-44
20. Jesus eats with a sinner and changes his lifestyle	Luke 19:1-10
21. Jesus uses a meal to symbolize his own sacrifice, our salvation	Matthew 26:17-19, 26-29
22. Jesus makes himself known to disciples after resurrection by breaking bread (1)	Luke 24:13-32
23. Jesus makes himself known to disciples after resurrection by breaking bread (2)	John 21:4-13
24. Early church shares food	Acts 2:42
25. First church controversy: food	Acts 6:1-6
26. God uses food to instruct Peter to evangelize Gentiles	Acts 10:1-35
27. Food becomes an ethical issue	1 Corinthians 10:14-24
28. The Supper of the Lamb: the consummation of all things	Revelation 19:6-9

5

Type: Quiz
Time: 5-8 minutes

Meals Jesus Ate

Eating and drinking for Jesus were times when he talked, fellowshiped, celebrated, and ministered. He ate and drank with people so frequently and zestily that his enemies accused him of gluttony! (See Luke 7:34.) At least fifteen of his meals are mentioned in the four Gospels. Remembering them, we can remember also that we work to erase world hunger so that all persons may know the joys that come from eating well of God's bounty with their families and friends.

MATERIALS NEEDED: Procedure A — none, or a chalkboard, chalk
Procedure B — paper, pencils for all

PROCEDURES: Procedure A — Ask participants to call out as many meals of Jesus as they remember. You may write them on a chalkboard for reference later if you wish. If not, keep count so the group can see how good their corporate memory is.

Procedure B — Ask each participant to list as many meals as s/he can. You might offer a table hunger bank as a prize for the best list. (See page 136).

VARIATIONS: Use the meals of Jesus to draw a mural (see "Following Food Through the Bible," page 24).
Play "Twenty Questions" with these.

POSSIBLE ANSWERS:

1. At the home of Matthew (Matthew 9:10)
2. Ate corn on Sabbath (Matthew 12:1)
3. Fed 5,000 (Matthew 14:13-21)
4. Fed 4,000 (Matthew (15:32-38)

26

5. Anointed while eating (Matthew 26:6 or John 12:2-3)*
6. Eating with a Pharisee when woman washed feet (Luke 7:36)*
7. Passover—Last Supper (Matthew 26:20 ff.)
8. At Mary and Martha's home (Luke 10:38-42)
9. Eating with Pharisee when he did not wash (Luke 11:37)
10. Eating with Pharisees, discussed Sabbath cures (Luke 14:1-24)
11. Eating with Zacchaeus (Luke 19:5)
12. Eating with disciples at Emmaus (Luke 24:13, 30)
13. Eating with disciples in Jerusalem after resurrection (Luke 24:42)
14. Wedding at Cana (John 2:1-11)
15. Ate in Samaria; disciples went to buy food (John 4)
16. Breakfast on the beach (John 21:9)
17. Possibly in Peter's home** (Mark 1:30-31)

---

* Probably the same incident
** The scripture says Peter's mother-in-law waited on Jesus; tradition implies a meal.

6

Meals Jesus Ate — Placemat

Using the Meals Jesus Ate on the previous page, print up placemats for church suppers that diners can complete before or after a meal. You might copy the introduction from page 26 and ask "How many can you name?" Decorate with Christian food symbols; suggestions below.

MEALS JESUS ATE

How many can you name?

1.	9.
2.	10.
3.	11.
4.	12.
5.	13.
6.	14.
7.	15.
8.	16.

7

Type: Scripture Analysis
Time: Open

The Debate

Jesus once declared, "'Blessed are you who are in need; the kingdom of God is yours.'" (Luke 6:20) From that we might conclude that God loves the poor very much. But do the poor believe that? Especially the poor who have no knowledge about Jesus except what well-fed, well-dressed Western Christians have told them? And do affluent Christians really believe God loves the poor as much as or even more than the rich? What can we say? The purpose of this game is to open up our own attitudes and to explore them together.

PROCEDURE:
1. Divide participants into two teams. Designate one team the Hungry Non-Christians, the other the Well-fed Christians.

2. Let each team caucus for 5 minutes to come up with arguments on the question: "Does God really love the poor?" The Hungry side should argue no and come up with reasons to support their position; the well-fed side should argue yes, and come up with reasons to support their position.

3. Let every participant pair off with a member of the opposite team for a 10-minute debate. You may also want to stage a panel debate, using two team members from each side, with a moderator.

4. Discuss as a whole group which arguments on both sides made the most sense. Did any of them challenge the group's own Christian witness?

29

8

Type: Art Work
Time: Open

Parable Put-ups

Many times Jesus illustrated his teachings with references to food. Sometimes he taught that what we do with food has a direct bearing on our eternal destiny. This exercise asks participants to choose one saying or parable to meditate on and illustrate.

You may ask them to create posters, banners, collages, or cartoons, and provide appropriate materials. You might even award prizes and use creations to decorate a room, fellowship hall, or sanctuary.

SUGGESTED THEMES:

"Man shall not live by bread alone" (Matthew 4:4)

"You are the salt of the earth" (Matthew 5:13)

"Blessed are you that hunger now, for you shall be satisfied"
(Luke 6:21)

"Give us this day our daily bread" (Matthew 6:11)

"A sound tree cannot bear evil fruit" (Matthew 7:18)

"I am the vine, you are the branches" (John 15:5)

"If you have faith as a grain of mustard seed . . . " (Matthew 17:20)

"I will make you fishers of men" (Matthew 4:19)

"The kingdom of heaven is like a grain of mustard seed"
(Matthew 13:31-32)

"The kingdom of heaven is like leaven" (Matthew 13:33)

"I am the bread of life" (John 6:35)

SUGGESTED PARABLES TO ILLUSTRATE:

Rich man and Lazarus (Luke 16:19-31)

The last judgment (Matthew 25:31-46)

The prodigal son's return (Luke 15:11-24)

Feasting in the kingdom (Luke 14:15-24)

The sower (Matthew 13:3-8)

Wheat and tares (Matthew 13:24-30)

Fishing net (Matthew 13:47-50)

9

Parable Placemats

Using some of the themes suggested in the previous game, print up placemats for church suppers that diners can complete before or after eating. At the top you might include an introduction such as:

Jesus frequently illustrated his teachings with references to food. Choose one of the following and illustrate it.

You are the salt of the earth.
(Matt. 5:13)

I am the vine, you are the branches.
(John 6:35)

I am the bread of life.
(John 15:5)

I will make you fishers of men.
(Matt. 4:19)

A sound tree cannot bear bad fruit.
(Matt. 7:18, N.E.B.)

The kingdom of heaven is like yeast . . .
(Matt. 13:33, N.E.B.)

PARABLE PLACEMAT

10

Scripture Mini-skits

Scripture mini-skits are Bible stories acted out briefly with no props and little or no rehearsal. Lines come directly from scripture, augmented by imaginative ad libs, and action is minimal.

Mini-skits have many uses, among them:

as a family method of Bible study

as a lively opening for a church night supper, church school class, or hunger workshop

as an imaginative presentation of scripture during worship.

Mini-skits can also be performed in pantomine as scripture charades.

Three gospel stories concerning hunger are especially adaptable for mini-skits:

The feeding of the 5000 (John 6:3-13)*

Lazarus and the rich man (Luke (16:19-31)**

The last judgment (Matthew 25:31-46)

SUGGESTIONS FOR EFFECTIVE MINI-SKITS:

1. Use a narrator to begin the skit by reading the Biblical introduction. Narrator may also read or tell connecting parts of the story.
2. Actors won't need much rehearsal, but should be thoroughly familiar with the story so they can recite or paraphrase lines.
3. Humor is appreciated by most audiences. It adds zest and makes a story come alive.
4. If used as charades, mini-skits should be given elaborate actions so audiences can understand them without words.
5. Some groups have "modernized" these stories effectively, setting the feeding of the 5000 in a crusade stadium, and interpreting Lazarus and the rich man as rich and poor nations.

---

* To make this story even more effective, add one character: a man or woman who has a picnic basket but doesn't offer it because it seems too little. Show his or her shame when Jesus takes even less and makes it into more than enough.

** If children are in the group, be sure you include dogs and angels as characters—they love to play these parts!

11

Type: Scripture Analysis
Time: 10-20 minutes

Letter from Beyond

The story of Lazarus and the rich man found in Luke 16:19-31 is one of Jesus' most disturbing parables. It is also one of his most graphic on the subject of feeding the poor. This game asks participants to imagine they are the rich man who has been given permission to write one letter from beyond the grave to his brothers on earth. Allow time afterwards for discussion.

MATERIALS NEEDED: A Bible, pen, and sheet of 8 x 10 paper per person.

PROCEDURE:
1. Read the story aloud.

2. Ask participants to read it again to themselves, seeing themselves as the rich man. Tell them they have been given permission to write one letter to brothers on earth.

3. Allow 5 - 10 minutes for letter writing.

4. Let all who will share their letters with the group.

5. Discuss such questions as these:

   a) What does this parable have to say to us as the world's wealthiest people?

   b) If Lazarus is seen as a poor nation and the rich man as a rich nation, what might it say to us?

   c) If Lazarus is seen as a poor church and the rich man as an affluent church, what might it say to us?

   d) If Lazarus is seen as humanity hungry for the word of God and the rich man is seen as Christians with that word, what might it say to us?

33

12

Type: Board Game
Time: 5-15 minutes

Bible Picture Lotto

Small children need a way to learn what the Bible says about God's care for the poor and hungry, too. Most games which require reading skills leave them out, but here is one designed especially with non-readers in mind.

PREPARE BEFOREHAND: Game board for each child or each two children.

1. Select ten pictures from church school literature of Jesus helping someone (especially good: feeding five thousand, last supper, healing, holding a child). Each of these must have a duplicate, since this is a matching activity.

2. Glue each of the cut-out pictures to posterboard or construction paper to make them firm. The background pieces should all be the same size (3½ x 4" is a good size).

3. To prepare the game board, take a piece of lightweight posterboard large enough to hold all twenty pictures with spaces between. With a marking pen, outline spaces for all 20 pictures, four rows of five. On the second and fourth rows, glue one set of ten pictures. (See illustration.)

4. For durability, cover the duplicate pictures with clear contact paper.

(Adapted from Picture Lotto, which was developed by Brethren House Ministries, St. Petersburg, Florida. Picture Lotto appears on page 68.)

34

PROCEDURE: For one player, stack the individual picture cards in front of the player and ask the child to match them with the cards glued on the board. To increase learning, you might ask the child to explain to you what is going on in each picture as s/he matches it.

For two players, make two games boards for five pictures each. Stack the ten matching cards face down between the players. Each in turn looks at a picture. If the picture matches one on his/her board, it goes in the appropriate space. If it belongs to the other, it is turned over beside the stack. Playing continues until one player has matched all the spaces on his/her board. To increase learning, let each player tell the other what is going on in pictures as they are matched.

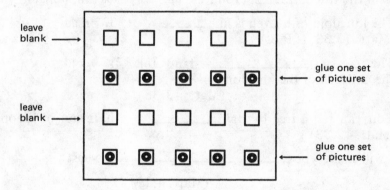

35

13

Type: Quiz
Time: 5 minutes

He Said It!

(Reproduce a copy for each participant.)

Jesus often talked about food. In fact, if we deleted all his references to food and money, we would have very few teachings left! Below are some food teachings. How many can you complete?

1. You are the _____ of the earth. (Matt. 5:13)

   a. fruit

2. Woe to you who are _____, for you shall _____. (Luke 6:25)

   b. vine

3. I am the _____ of life. (John 6:35)

   c. mustard seed

4. [People do] not live by _____ alone. (Matt. 4:4)

   d. salt

5. I am the true _____. (John 15:1)

   e. full, hunger

6. The kingdom of heaven is like _____. (Matt. 13:33, N.E.B.)

   f. bread

7. The _____ _____ stands for the children of the kingdom. (Matt. 13:38)

   g. bread

8. You can tell a tree by its _____. (Matt. 12:33)

   h. fishers of [people]

9. I will make you _____ _____ _____. (Matt. 4:19)

   i. yeast

10. If you have faith no bigger than a _____ _____, you can move mountains. (Matt. 17:20, N.E.B.)

    j. good seed

PROCEDURE: Use this quiz to spark a discussion or begin a study of hunger by pointing out that just as Jesus knew food is important, so we, too, know it is important. Jesus fed the minds, hearts, and bodies of the hungry. If we follow him, how can we neglect any of the three?

Answers: 1. d; 2. e; 3. f; 4. g; 5. b; 6. i; 7. j; 8. a; 9. h; 10. c

36

14

Type: Drama
Time: 8-12 minutes

Unto One of the Least

by Dorothy J. Collins

CHARACTERS:* Jane — an active churchwoman
Henry — her husband
Long-haired youth seeking work
Older man — city maintenance employee
Disheveled woman
Off-stage voice for the Lord

PROPS: Chair, table, couch if available (or chairs put together), loaf of bread, empty glass jar, broom, welcome mat, old tattered robe, raincoat, basket, bakery box.

SCENE: Jane and Henry's home, represented by the couch, chair and table. The loaf of bread and jar are on the table, the robe is slung across the chair, the broom leans nearby and the welcome mat is off to one side to indicate a door.

(Stage lights high.)

(Enter Jane, wearing raincoat and carrying bakery box. As she begins to speak she sets the box on the table, takes off her raincoat and drapes it across the back of the chair, picks up the broom, and begins to sweep the room.)

JANE: I sure didn't think that meeting would take so long over at church. Now I haven't much time to straighten up around here and get supper ready before Henry comes home. *(Begins singing.)*

---

* Be as representative as possible of various ethnic groups.

©1975, Dorothy J. Collins. Used by permission.

37

What the world needs now is love, sweet love . . . *(Knock at the door.)* Come in!

(Enter long-haired youth.)

YOUTH: Pardon me, lady. Do you have any work I could do for you? I'm trying to earn some money. Maybe I could wash some windows or cut the grass?

JANE: No, I can't think of anything that needs doing right now. Besides, I'm very busy myself.

YOUTH: Gee, I haven't been able to find any steady work and I haven't had anything to eat since yesterday morning.

JANE: Well, I'm sorry to hear that, but I don't have a job for you. Wait a minute, though, maybe I could give you something to eat. Let's see . . . *(Picks up the cake box, speaks to herself.)* No, I don't want to cut this cake before Henry comes home. *(To the youth.)* Look, no one eats the crusts around here anyway. If you are really hungry, this ought to tide you over. *(Gives him the ends from the loaf of bread. He takes them and begins to back out the door.)*

YOUTH: Thank you, lady. Sorry to bother you. *(Leaves.)*

JANE: Okay. *(Calls after him.)* Hey! Why don't you get a haircut? Then maybe someone would hire you. *(Returns to sweeping and singing)* What the world needs now is love, sweet love . . . *(Another knock. She calls out, exasperated.)* Come in!

(Enter the older man, mopping his brow.)

MAN: Excuse me, ma'am. I'm with the city street department, and I'm fixing the hole in the street at the end of your driveway.

JANE: Good! It's about time that was fixed.

MAN: Well, ma'am, it's very hot out there, and I'm real thirsty. If it's no trouble, could I have a drink of water?

JANE: Good grief, all these interruptions! I'll never get any of *my* work done. Here, take this jar and go around back. There's a tap there. Drink all you want, but don't bother me anymore.

38

MAN: Thank you, ma'am. Sorry to trouble you.

JANE: *(Returns to sweeping, muttering to herself.)* He ought to carry a jug of water with him. I've a notion to bring in the welcome mat. Look at the time! I have *got* to get this house dusted before Henry gets home. *(Begins to sing again "What the world needs now" and reaches for the old robe, starts to tear it up for dustcloths. There is another knock at the door.)* Now what??? Come in!

(Woman enters, weeping hysterically. Her clothers are in shreds and she clutches them about her body. Her hair is a mess.)

JANE: Who are you? What happened?

WOMAN: *(Sobbing.)* Please, oh please, help me. When I left the shopping center a man grabbed me. He shoved me into his car and drove me to some woods. *(Sobs again.)* He tore off my clothes and assaulted me! *(Sobs.)* Then he drove me back here and pushed me out at the corner. This was the nearest house. Oh please, please help me!

JANE: For heaven's sake. I can't believe all this. Look, dear, now I hope you understand, but I really don't want to get involved in this. But we must do something to cover you up. *(Grabs her raincoat, then says to herself.)* No, not my good raincoat. *(Picks up the old robe, says to the woman.)* Here, I was going to use this old robe for a dust rag anyway. You take it! *(Places robe around the distraught woman and ushers her to the door.)* Now, dear, don't you worry. I've got an idea. A policeman lives just three doors to your left. Why don't you go there for help? I'm really sorry about what happened to you, but I'm sure you understand about my not wanting to get involved.

WOMAN: Will you at least come with me to the policeman's house? That man might still be out there!

JANE: Oh dear! No, I couldn't possibly go with you. Just run. Now good luck, dear.

(The woman leaves reluctantly. Jane picks up the welcome mat and drops it by the table, then paces the floor.)

JANE: I can't believe it. All these strangers and their problems. Why did they all come here?

39

(Enter Henry.)

HENRY: Hi, honey, I'm home.

JANE: *(Falls into his arms. Gasps.)* Thank goodness it's you, Henry.

HENRY: Why, Jane, you're upset. What on earth has happened?

JANE: Well, first I spent all morning in mission meetings at the church. But this afternoon . . . you can't imagine what I've been through. There's been a bunch of beggars in the neighborhood, and they've all been *here,* bugging me. I finally had to bring in the welcome mat.

HENRY: *(Puzzled.)* Beggars? In this neighborhood? Begging for what?

JANE: First a hippy wanted food. Then some guy was thirsty. And to top it all off, a woman showed up practically naked, crying because some man attacked her. Oh, Henry! *(She clutches her chest.)*

HENRY: Now, Jane, take it easy. *(Walks her to the couch.)* What did you do about the woman?

JANE: I told her that I really didn't want to get involved, and I sent her to the policeman down the street. Henry, do you realize that man may still be running around loose? I hope they catch him, and he rots in prison. It's just so much excitement, Henry. I . . . I can't take it. Oh, oh! *(Collapses on couch.)*

HENRY: *(Grabs her.)* Jane? Jane! Oh, dear, she's fainted. *(Feels her pulse.)* Oh, no! I believe she's dead! I must get help! *(Rushes from the stage.)*

(Stage lights out. Offstage, the bread crust, empty jar and old robe have been placed in a basket, which is now brought in and placed beside Jane.)

(Stage lights on low, preferably a soft spot on Jane.)

OFF-STAGE VOICE: Jane? Jane.

(Jane rouses and sits up slowly. Looks about her.)

JANE: Who's that? *(Silence.)* Lord? Lord, is that you? *(Silence. She looks around.)* Why, I do believe I've died and gone

40

to heaven. *(Spots basket, picks it up and puts it beside) her.)* What's this? Maybe it's my heavenly reward. They talked about that in church. I wonder what I've got? *(One at a time and very slowly she lifts out each article and holds it up, staring at it in bewilderment.)* A crust of bread? *(Pause.)* An empty jar? *(Pause.)* MY OLD ROBE?

OFF-STAGE VOICE: *(Slowly and emphatically.)* Verily I say unto you, in as much as you have done it unto one of the least of these . . .

(Lights out.)

THE END

fact-finding games

The games, quizzes, skits, and surveys found in this section teach basic facts about hunger at home and around the world. Most of them let participants *do* something with one or more basic hunger facts so these facts come alive. After each of these games participants need a few minutes to discuss what they have learned and experienced before moving on.

Contents

*In minutes (approximate)

15

Type: Survey
Time: 10-15 minutes

What Do We Need to Know?

The purpose of this exercise is to call forth from a group facts they already know about hunger in order to avoid studying something unnecessarily and to identify areas they need to study.

MATERIALS NEEDED: Paper and pencil for each participant.

PROCEDURE: (a) Ask the group to list individually for two minutes all the words and phrases that come to mind when "hunger" is mentioned.

(b) Call time. Ask them to put a check (✓) by any items they feel they know something about, and two checks by any items they know a good deal about. (1 minute)

(c) Ask them to circle 3 to 5 items they feel they need to know more about. (1-2 minutes)

(d) Finally ask them to complete the following sentence: "My greatest question about hunger is . . . "

Either share answers as a group, or turn them in to a planning group for tabulation and study/action planning.

16

Type: Poster or Simulation
Time: 30 seconds

Eye Examination

This is a dramatic way to teach the effects of hunger on vision.

PREPARE BEFOREHAND: A large poster in block letters to resemble an eye chart (see artwork below). The top line should be quite large, with each line decreasing in size until the bottom line is barely readable.

PROCEDURE: Either singly or as a group, inform participants they are to be given a vision test. Ask participants to stand behind a line (or hold the "chart" up in front of them) and ask them to read the chart covering their right eye, then their left. Follow the examination with a discussion of the fact.

THE
PRESIDENT'S
COMMISSION ON WORLD
HUNGER REPORTED IN 1980 THAT
100,000 CHILDREN IN THE WORLD THIS YEAR
WILL GO BLIND SIMPLY FOR A LACK OF VITAMIN A

45

17

Type: Quiz
Time: 3-5 minutes

Just Imagine It!

(Reproduce one for each participant or ask questions aloud and let group answer.)

Imagine what you and I would have to do to move from our country to any one of the world's poorest countries . . . countries like Lesotho, Paraguay, Chad, Afghanistan, Bangladesh. Can you imagine it? Below are some questions about how you would live. How accurately can you picture it?

1. Your home would be approximately as large as an American
   (a) house (b) garage (c) toolshed (d) doghouse

2. Which of the following furniture would you probably have?
   (a) a table, chairs, bed, one chest
   (b) a table and one chair, a few blankets
   (c) a table, no chairs, a bed and no chest
   (d) a table and chairs, stove, bed and chest

3. Your family wardrobe could consist of
   (a) one outfit per person, shoes for the head of the family
   (b) two outfits per person, including shoes
   (c) one outfit per person, no shoes
   (d) a few worn garments

4. In your pantry you'd probably have
   (a) dried meat and a few vegetables
   (b) a little flour, salt and sugar, mouldy potatoes, dried beans, onions
   (c) only rice
   (d) dried meat, vegetables, powdered milk

Based on Chapter 11 of Robert L. Heilbroner's *The Great Ascent* (Harper and Row, 1963).

46

5. You would get water from

   (a) a spigot in your yard   (b) the village well   (c) a river

6. You would probably own

   (a) electric lights (b) a pet dog (c) a saw (d) no tools or pets

7. You would get information from

   (a) magazines (b) your radio (c) your TV (d) the village radio

8. When you got sick, you would go to

   (a) the doctor down the street
   (b) a clinic 10 miles away, run by a midwife
   (c) the hospital in the next town
   (d) heaven

9. Your annual income would average

   (a) $100 – $300
   (b) $500 – $1000
   (c) $1000 – $3000
   (d) $3000 – $5000

10. Your expectancy would probably be

   (a) about the same as now
   (b) 5-10 years less
   (c) 25-30 years less
   (d) 5-10 years more

Answers: 1-c; 2-b; 3-a; 4-b; 5-b; 6-d; 7-d; 8-b; 9-a; 10-c

47

18

Type: Survey
Time: 15-30 minutes

A Self-survey:
Basic Factual and Value Choices

The world hunger crisis is both easy to understand and complex. Put simply, someone will starve to death today and we have the resources to do something about it. Nearly everyone agrees with these two factual claims.

Complexity and disagreement arise about whether we should act, and if so, what we should do.

Should we be proud of our own food reserves and wonder why others are incapable of feeding themselves? Should we blame ourselves or American foreign policy and call for an American disengagement from world-mindedness? Should we rush emergency food? Do we know how to overcome the obstacles which have caused many previous aid programs to fail? What are the related goals which must be achieved to obtain security against famine and hunger for the first time in history?

This self-survey highlights basic factual questions and introduces different attitudinal and value choices. It is designed to help you understand the problem, different attitudes toward it, and alternative policies being considered.

(Reproduce one for each participant.)

BASIC FACTUAL JUDGMENTS:

Different views of the facts concerning the current hunger crisis help explain why some people favor a short-term emergency program while others favor no program at all and still others believe only a long-term reordering of the international economic order will suffice. Oddly enough, the belief that there is no problem and the belief that it is overwhelmingly large often lead to the same lack of response. In addition, the numbers opposed to a response are increased by those who recognize a problem, but deny that we can or should do anything about it. What is your judgment?

Is there a problem? Should we respond? How?

Reprinted and updated by permission from the *World Hunger Crisis Kit*, Robert Woito (Editor), World Without War Publications, 1975. (See Additional Resources List.) New data from the *Preliminary Report* of the Presidential Commission on World Hunger, December, 1979.

48

1. What percent of the world's population are hungry or under-nourished?
   a. 5%   b. 10%   c. 25%   d. 50%

2. How many small children will die this year from malnutrition-related causes?
   a. 1 million   c. 5-10 million
   b. 3-5 million   d. 12-15 million

3. The average per capita wealth (Gross National Product)
   A. in the United States is more than
      a. $2000 b. $3000 c. $5000 d. $6000

   B. in other developed countries
      a. $3000 b. $4000 c. $5000 d. $6000

   C. in the 40 poorest countries
      a. $100   b. $200   c. $300   d. $400

   D. in other developing countries
      a. $100   b. $200   c. $300   d. $400

4. The difference between average life expectancy in developed countries and in developing countries is:
   a. 5 years   b. 10 years   c. 20 years   d. 30 years

5. U.S. per capita grain consumption when compared to the 40 least developed countries is:
   a. about the same per person   c. about 5 times as much
   b. about twice as much   d. about 10 times as much

6. Americans consume 90% of their grain indirectly as meat, milk, and eggs. If Americans were to reduce their beef consumption by one-third, or were to switch from grain-fed to grass-fed beef, enough grain would be freed for export to feed how many people?
   a. 1 million   c. 100 million
   b. 10 million   d. 250 million

7. Throughout the Third World as a whole, 80% of the farms are 12 acres or less. Over half that number are under
   a. 1 acre   b. 2.5 acres   c. 5 acres   d. 10 acres

8. Past trends indicate that global grain production will be able to keep up with the projected *commercial demand* for food. How-ever, to meet the needs of persons unable to pay for their food (through special feeding programs) the Food and Agriculture Organization estimates that by 1990 an additional how many metric tons of grain will be needed?
   a. 25   b. 32   c. 40   d. 50

9. Currently the world's population is approximately 4.2 billion. At present growth rates, by 2000 the world's estimated population will be

   a. 4.5 billion   b. 5 billion   c. 6 billion   d. 8 billion

10. Historically, which comes first:
   a. population control precedes the possibility of the capital accumulation needed for development
   b. economic development provides some assurance of survival which decreases the need for large families

---

Answers: 1-c; 2-d; 3. A-c; B-a; C-a; D-d; 4-c; 5-c; 6-c; 7-b; 8-b; 9-c; 10-b.

ATTITUDES AND VALUES:

If there is a world hunger crisis, what caused it? What values guide your response? What goals should this country seek?

There are no right or wrong answers to these questions. The choices given below express viewpoints presented in the current debate. Select the answer which comes *closest* to expressing your view.

11. How do you explain the existence of poverty and hunger on a massive global scale?

   a. Some cultures or economic systems are inherently incapable of promoting adequate production of food and other resources for their people.
   b. The rich capitalist countries exploit poorer developing nations and thus inhibit their ability to provide for their own people.
   c. There simply aren't enough resources to provide adequately for all the world's people and the uneven distribution of what we have is nature's fault, not ours.
   d. The resources exist, but the world community lacks the sense of commitment and the structures which would enable us to provide adequately for all the world's people.
   e. Other:

12. What basic values do you consider in deciding your response to the world hunger crisis?

   a. The religious obligation to help the poor.
   b. The well-being of the United States.
   c. The correction of past injustices.

50

d. A sense of world community.

e. Other:

13. If forced by population growth, the finiteness of the earth's resources, and the recognition that [people do] not live by bread alone, what policies would you advocate in a time when there is not enough:

a. Help no one, our own survival is at stake and the natural population stabilization forces of the earth's environment are at work.

b. Help those who are politically or strategically essential to our survival and who can benefit from such help.

c. Help everyone in danger of starvation.

d. We must do everything in our power to avoid such a terrible situation while there is still time.

e. Other:

14. In the effort to overcome world hunger and poverty, what do you believe is a worthwhile and attainable goal by the year 2000?

a. Equal distribution of wealth and resources among the world's people.

b. Achieving minimum standards of nutrition and livelihood necessary to assure a tolerable existence for all the world's people.

c. Continue to stave off massive starvation through emergency food aid programs, but don't expect to "solve" the problem of world hunger.

d. Do as much as we reasonably can, but expect many millions of people will die of starvation in the foreseeable future.

e. Other:

15. What do you think will be required to solve the problem of world hunger and poverty?

a. The elimination of exploitation of the poor by the rich and redistribution of the world's wealth.

b. An increased commitment by rich nations to aid poor nations in both emergency assistance and the achievement of economic development.

c. Development of new technology to increase food production.

d. The creation of international structures and processes capable of planning rationally to meet common global problems.

e. Reducing the rate of population growth in poor countries.

f. Placing constraints on the level of food, energy, and other resource consumption of the developed nations.

g. Other:

16. What do you think this country should be willing to do to help solve the problem of world hunger and poverty?

a. Increase agricultural production and food aid, but not at the expense of the American diet.

b. Increase food aid even though it would mean a reduction in American consumption.

c. Encourage and help subsidize increased food production capabilities in poor countries.

d. Take initiatives designed to build the international structures needed to deal multilaterally with the hunger crisis.

e. Other:

ACTORS AND POLICIES:

Who are the major individuals or organizations and political structures which must act to resolve the world hunger crisis? What are the policy areas in which change is needed? Indicate all you think apply.

17. Which of the following do you believe are important actors in eliminating world hunger?

a. the individual

b. non-governmental organizations (churches, labor unions, private relief organizations, business associations, etc.)

c. multi-national enterprises

d. the United States

e. every industrialized country

f. the oil producing countries

g. every country in the world

h. international organizations

i. transnational organizations

j. all of the above

k. Other:

18. Which of the following subjects should be studied to determine wise policies of aid in resolving the world hunger crisis?

a. the law of the sea, particularly the utilization of fish resources, mining of the sea bed resources and off-shore minerals

52

b. the global and regional arms races currently consuming over $200 billion every year
c. how to create a sense of community between hostile, even belligerent, people and nations
d. the utilization of the Oil Producing Export Countries' (OPEC) new economic wealth
e. the functioning of the International Monetary Fund
f. the patterns and rules of world trade
g. the strains on the earth's environment
h. different religious and ethical teachings concerning the obligations of the rich and the poor to each other
i. the degree of transnational cooperation likely and how it can be increased
j. paths to peace in the Middle East
k. the role of multi-national corporations and state enterprises involved in world financial transactions
l. population growth
m. the role of women in developing countries in improving nutritional content of food
n. labor intensive agricultural techniques
o. technology applicable to developing countries
p. decreasing erosion, increasing land under cultivation
q. improving crop yields through new high yield seeds, better fertilizers, and new farming techniques
r. the impact of pesticides on the environment and the possibilities of organic or natural pest control methods
s. converting sewage in the U.S. to safe, effective fertilizers
t. overcoming domestic hunger
u. decreasing grain feed for cattle, increasing grazing
v. land reform in developing countries
w. artificial foods and new energy sources
x. the formation of new raw material cartels, like OPEC
y. feasible changes in diet and lifestyles to consume less
z. all of the above

19

Type: Simulation
Time: 2-5 minutes

The Race

The purpose of this game is to demonstrate how each person's position in the "race of life" determines his or her ability to win in that race. *The reward for winning this game is food.* Each participant is asked to run, but most are given some arbitrary handicap, just as in the real game of life we are assigned where we are born, our physical bodies, etc. Because of the way the game is played, persons handicapped by forces outside themselves have little or no chance to win, while those given advantageous positions have a hard time losing.

This game also illustrates another hunger fact: that Americans annually consume 1850 pounds of grain per person, most of it used to feed livestock to produce the meat, milk, and eggs we eat. In contrast, the average African and Asian consumes about 400 pounds of grain a year, and that average is so unequally distributed that many starve or suffer permanent brain damage.

PREPARE BEFOREHAND: One sheet of paper labeled "First Prize: 1850 lbs. of grain" and a second labeled "Second Prize: _____ lbs. of grain." (Fill in the blank by multiplying 400 times the number of players minus one.)

MATERIALS NEEDED: Two prizes prepared ahead, a piece of chalk to mark starting and finish lines.

PROCEDURE: Place players at the starting line. Choose one player arbitrarily to be the American, and send him/her half-way toward the finish line to await the starting signal. Tell other players they are members of Third World countries.

The object of the game is to win the race. Be sure all players understand that! Those who don't get First Prize are entitled to as big a piece of Second Prize as they can tear off when they reach the finish line.

Then assign handicaps to most of the players from the Third World. Some players may move up between the starting line and the

54

American, but must run backwards. Some players must run sideways, some must hop on one foot, some must crawl, some must crawl backwards, and one player is not allowed to run at all.

As Game Director, blow a whistle or call "Ready, set, go!"

After the Race, let players discuss their feelings about what happened. You might use such questions as:

How did you feel about your assigned place? Did you think it was fair that you were where you were, with your handicap?

How did the Third World feel about the American? The American about the Third World?

Did you know ahead of time who would win? How did you feel?

How equally was 2nd prize divided? Why?

What dynamics might have prevented the American from winning first prize automatically?

Given that this race represents the real world food situation, how do we reflect on that race as inevitable winners?

Starve the Man

An old children's favorite, Hang the Man, has been turned into a hunger game called Starve the Man. The purpose of the game is to draw a picture of a starving man before other players can guess a word selected by the "artist." One line of the picture is added for each incorrect guess. The man is drawn as follows:

1. a bowl
2. hand and arm
3. body
4. leg
5. foot
6. head
7. eye
8. nose
9. mouth
10. tear

MATERIALS NEEDED: For two players, merely a pencil and paper. For a group, a chalkboard and chalk. You might also want to list "Causes of Hunger" and/or "Hungry Countries" for a group (see below).

PROCEDURE: The "artist" selects a word dealing with a cause for hunger or a hungry country, and draws blanks on the paper or chalkboard to indicate the number of letters in his/her word. The other players then must try to guess the word either by asking "Is there a (letter of the alphabet) in your word?" or by outright trying to guess the word. For each incorrect letter or word guessed, the artist can add a part to the starving man picture. If the word is guessed, the guesser becomes the next artist. If the word is not guessed before the picture is completed the artist gets another turn.

SUGGESTIONS FOR WORDS:

CAUSES OF HUNGER (related words)

weather conditions: drought, floods, rain, heat, cold, monsoons, hurricanes, earthquakes, etc.

natural disasters: poor seeds, insects, blight, bugs, worms, etc.

military spending: bombs, bullets, soldiers, war, budgets, etc.

trade laws: laws, politicians, greed, balance of trade, products, money, corporations, etc.

overpopulation: babies, people, mothers, fathers, elderly, etc.

illiteracy: no books, poor education, no education, etc.

land use: peasants, owners, rich, big farms, industrialization, etc.

urbanization: ghettos, slums, cities, unemployment, etc.

lifestyle: affluence, overconsumption, indifference, ignorance, television, junk foods, etc.

transportation: poor roads, trucks, regulations, etc.

(Note: These are only some of the causes of hunger. Your group may want to add others, and will certainly be able to add words to each list.)

HUNGRY COUNTRIES (a partial list*)

Algeria	Laos
Angola	Liberia
Bangladesh	Malawi
Bolivia	Malaysia
Botswana	Mauritania
Burma	Mozambique
Central African Republic	Nepal
Chad	North Korea
Colombia	North Vietnam
Congo	Philippines
Dominican Republic	Rwanda
Ecuador	Saudi Arabia
Gambia	Sierra Leone
Ghana	Somalia
Guinea	South Vietnam
Guyana	Sri Lanka
Haiti	Tanzania
India	Upper Volta
Indonesia	Zaire
Iran	Zambia

---

* Based on 1970 and 1972 data from the United Nations' Food and Agricultural Organization. Countries included average less than 55% of daily protein needs and less than 89% of daily calorie needs.

57

21

Geography Lesson U.S.A.

Sometimes we are tempted to think that hunger exists only in the rest of the world, but not in our own country. Yet certain situations and groups of Americans are as hungry as if they lived in the third world. While their income level is well above those of third world residents, it is not high enough to permit them to live above a subsistence level in our own country. This game helps remind us of who and where they are.

PREPARE BEFOREHAND: Either a large outline map of the U.S.A. or small maps for each participant. (For a permanent game, make a flannel board instead.) Using the illustration below, place symbols in proper places.

PROCEDURE: Inform participants that this is a "Third World Map" of the U.S.A.—that this map shows where hungry persons live and who they are in our society. Ask them, either as a group or individually, to identify each symbolized group.

VARIATIONS: (a) This makes a good placemat for a hunger or church night meal.

(b) With a flannel board and small group, you might ask teams to construct the map rather than identify groups.

(c) You might want also to make a more detailed map of your own state's hungry.

This game is useful to introduce a discussion of Christian citizen responsibility to wipe out hunger at home, to introduce a program on any one aspect of U.S. hunger, or to lead into a planning session on "What Can We Do?"

MAP SHOULD SHOW (AT LEAST):

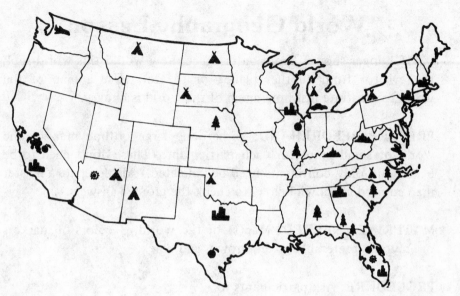

KEY:

🏭 — Urban poor

⚙ — Senior citizens

🐾 — Unemployed, especially in industry

🌲 — Rural poor

🍇 — Migrant workers

⛺ — Native Americans

⛰ — Mountain poor

22

World Geography Lesson

If hunger showed from outer space, how would this world look to a visitor from another planet—or to God? Use a map of the world to illustrate just how much of the world is hungry.

PREPARE BEFOREHAND: Either one large outline map of the world or small maps for each participant. (These don't need to be exact, and only continents need be indicated.) Also prepare a master map colored as shown below, to check the group's answers.

MATERIALS NEEDED: Map(s) of the world, 3 colors of markers or crayons—preferably green, brown, and black.

PROCEDURE: Ask participants to

(a) color *green* those areas of the world where most people are well-fed or overfed;

(b) color *brown* areas of the world where the population as a whole is adequately but not abundantly fed;

(c) color *black* areas of the world where a majority of the people are hungry or even starving.

Compare maps with one another (or discuss the larger map) before checking answers against the master. How accurately did the group see the world? Note the North-South division of hunger/affluence. How does this map compare with a map we might draw indicating the "most Christian" areas of the world? What might that comparison lead us to conclude? (You might use this to lead into a study of Matthew 25:31-46.)

60

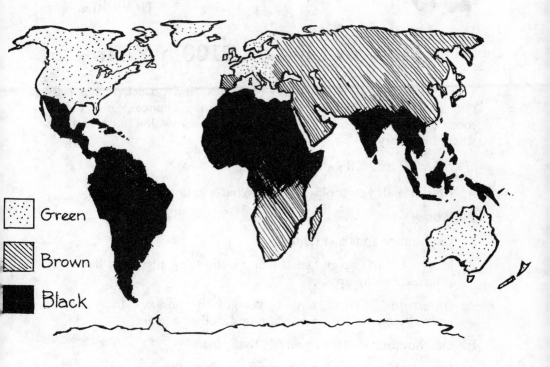

Green

Brown

Black

MAPS SHOULD SHOW:

Green

U.S.A. and Canada
Western Europe *except*
    Spain and Portugal
Australia, New Zealand
Japan

Brown

U.S.S.R. and Eastern Europe
China
Spain/Portugal
Middle East*
Southern Africa*

Black

India
Caribbean Islands
Southeast Asia
Northern Africa
    (over half the continent)
Latin America*

---

*Might place green dots over the brown or black to indicate a few persons are extremely well-fed while others starve.

61

23

Type: Drama
Time: 10 minutes

How to Live on $100 a Year

This skit requires no props, no costumes, and no set. It has only two characters, and can be performed in a chancel, in a family room or in a classroom. For youth groups, use dialog in parentheses where necessary.

(Two people meet. B looks downcast.)

A: Hey, friend, you look troubled. What's your problem?

B: Money.

A: Can't make ends meet, huh?

B: Meet? I can't even get them in shouting distance. The way prices are going up . . .

A: *(Interrupts.)* Friend, have I ever got the program for you! It's called "How to live on one hundred dollars a year."

B: One hundred dollars a *year?* Is that possible?

A: Sure. Half the people in the world do it all the time.

B: How do I start?

A: First, get rid of all your furniture except one table and one chair. That cuts down not only on payments, but also on cleaning supplies.

B: Cuts down on guests, too, But where do I sit to watch TV?

A: No TV, no radio, no books, or magazines. You're cutting down, remember.

B: Yeah, but . . . well, I guess I go out for my entertainment?

A: If you like. But give away all your clothes except one outfit— your oldest. And keep one pair of shoes for the head of the family.

Based on pamphlet number 103-2-1093, "How to Live on $100 a Year" distributed by the American Baptist Churches U.S.A.

B. You mean everybody else goes barefoot? The kids (I) might like that for a while, but I don't know about making it a regular practice. What else?

A: Shut off your electricity, water, and gas. Think of all the money you'll save! And disconnect the phone—don't forget that.

B: How will we run the dishwasher, toaster, hairdryer?

A: Send those to Goodwill. You can't afford them on one hundred dollars a year. And as for baths, use the rain.

B: How will we cook?

A: Gather scraps of wood and things that will burn. It's amazing how much waste wood you can find if you try. But donate most of your food to a crisis center. Keep only a small bag of flour, some sugar and salt, a few mouldy potatoes, a handful of onions, and some dried beans. Meal planning becomes a breeze!

B: *(Doubtfully.)* Is that a balanced diet?

A: Friend, on one hundred dollars a year, you can't have everything.

B: But what if I get sick? I can't even call a doctor—no phone.

A: Use the midwife in a clinic about ten miles away. Half the world does. And if you need a doctor, there's one further down the road.

B: How long would it take to *get* to a doctor—driving, I mean?

A: Driving? Oh—I forgot. You'll need to give up your car. They eat up your income.

B: *(Sarcastic.)* What'll we do with the garage—rent it out?

A: No, live in it. Get rid of the house, too. Of course your garage is larger than the ordinary house allowed in this program, but since you don't have a toolshed . . .

B: Hey, this isn't living, it's . . . What do I do about my job (school)? I can't walk there on an empty stomach, in my oldest clothes without a bath, and expect them to let me stay very long. I suppose this program thought of that, too?

A: Sure. Your best bet is to become a tenant farmer. With three acres and a good year, you can expect from one to three hundred dollars' worth of cash crops. Pay the landlord a third and the money lender ten percent, and you get what's left.

B: Money lender? Oh, come on. Why do I need a money lender?

A: Well, some years there'll be a drought, or maybe a flood. Then you won't get a hundred dollars. And you *need* a hundred dollars to live on this program effectively.

B: Yeah, I can see I do. What about saving for my old age?

A: Well, there's bad news and good news. You can't afford insurance, pension plans, or savings accounts, which is bad news. But the good news is that you won't need them.

B: Yeah? Why not?

A: Because under this program you can count on living twenty-five to thirty years less.

B: Oh, that's great. Hey, look, forget it, okay? I appreciate your trying to help and all, but suddenly I don't think I need help after all. My bills look pretty small. *(Starts to walk away and mutters to self.)* That's not living. It's barely existing. In fact, I'm not sure people *could* live like that *(Exits)*

A: *(Turns from B to audience and addresses them.)* Millions do. As I said before, half the people in our world live on this program year in and year out. They didn't choose it, but they're stuck with it.

In our economy we can't really live on a hundred dollars a year. But could we live on a hundred dollars a year *less?* That's about nine dollars a month, or two dollars a week. Would that require sacrifice? Would we even miss it? Yet think what could be done for the world's hungry if each person or even each family in this room gave a hundred dollars a year to fight hunger. Shall we?

(May be followed by a time of pledging or an offering.)

64

24

Type: Artwork
Time: Open

Advertising

This activity lets children and young teens become involved in advertising both the needs of the poor and possibilities for helping. It is especially effective as a way to involve them in promoting a special hunger offering or project.

MATERIALS NEEDED: Long strips of paper or cardboard to accommodate large-lettered sentences and slogans, crayons or marking pens, construction paper, scissors, and glue. (To help young printers, cardboard letter models and a 3" high roll of lined oak tag sentence strips are available in school supply stores.)

PROCEDURE: Display catchy slogans based on facts about world hunger, scripture verses, or other admonitions. Participants are asked to select any of the slogans and reproduce them on the long strips, either writing free-hand or tracing around cardboard letter models. They can also illustrate them if desired. Be sure strips are high enough and long enough to be read from a distance—12" high and 36" or longer is a good size.

SUGGESTED SLOGANS: Hunger is a Real Thing.

You can help.

"Feed the hungry." – JESUS

Created by Brethren House Ministries, 6301 56 Avenue N., St. Petersburg, Florida, 33709. Used by permission.

65

25

World Hunger View Crossword

How much do you know about hunger—its causes, results, and location? This crossword puzzle gives a quick view of world hunger. Every word in it except one relates in some way to hunger issues. Use it individually, as a class, or even as placemats for a hunger meal. (Answers on page 69.)

This particular crossword puzzle was put together by my mom and dad, Eddis and Sam Houck, and me one hot Sunday night, using our Scrabble board and extra letters made from paper. When you've worked this one, why not try to make up a puzzle of your own?

66

Across

1. These nations drain world resources
4. What many nations buy instead of bread
8. Many Christians see one of these and think they've "done something" about world hunger
9. What the world turns when the hungry speak: deaf _____
12. Part of Asia where hunger is great (abbrev.)
13. One who is hungry is also often _____
14. They can't read directions for planting crops or preparing food
16. These pests often infest the poor
17. Agency for International Development (initials)
19. They make up less of the world's population, consume most goods
21. World legislative body that works on hunger concerns (initials)
22. Family member missing in many hungry families
23. That is . . . (Lat. abbrev.)
30. Kissinger, for one
31. African nation recovering from aftermaths of political wars
32. U.S. organization that fights hunger with food packages
34. Part of Brazil that's most hungry
35. What hungry people often lack (abbrev.)
37. Unfavorable balance of this keeps countries poor
39. Another word for the world's hungry masses
40. One method of transportation in Arab countries
42. Sun deity in ancient Egypt, often held responsible for harvest
43. We use enough grain to produce this to feed 100 million a year!
44. Close sister of hunger

Down

1. A hungry continent
2. What crops did after drought
3. Nation crucial to solving hunger (initials)
4. An unstable economic one can cause hunger
5. He may exact a percent of wages from the poor
6. This rate must be slowed before hunger is wiped out
7. They eat stored grain
9. Measure of cloth used by village cooperative
10. Common man's name in some hungry lands
11. They own the land; the poor only work it
15. Cash crop in many hungry countries
18. How the eyes of hungry children look
20. What hungry nations must do with one another for trade
22. Illness that sweeps a country
24. When this African river doesn't flood, many go hungry
25. Natural cause of world hunger
26. Used for plowing in many lands
27. What village co-ops often make to sell, becoming self-reliant
28. Although hunger seems far away, actually it is very _____
29. One transportation route for getting crops to market
32. Great energy guzzlers, use up the world's petroleum
33. Hunger is a _____ that must be solved!
36. Word describing 7 down, 16 across
37. Zone where food grows most plentifully (abbrev.)
38. Syllable used by one who didn't hear the hungry man's question
41. Morsel left at a meal (with these in America we could feed millions)

67

26

Picture Lotto

This game is designed for very young children, non-readers, especially. It helps them learn about the work of one or more relief agencies.

PREPARE BEFOREHAND: A game board (or two, for two players—see procedure below).

1. Select ten pictures of relief projects, either from one agency or from several. You can find these in church literature, or in agency brochures. Each picture must have a duplicate, since this is a matching activity.

2. Glue one set of the cut-out pictures to posterboard or construction paper to make them firm. The background pieces should all be the same size (3½" x 4" is a good size).

3. To prepare the game board, use a piece of posterboard large enough to hold all twenty pictures allowing spaces between. With a marking pen, outline spaces for all 20 pictures, four rows of five. On the second and fourth rows, glue the duplicate set of pictures. (See illustration.)

4. For durability, cover the matching pictures with clear contact paper.

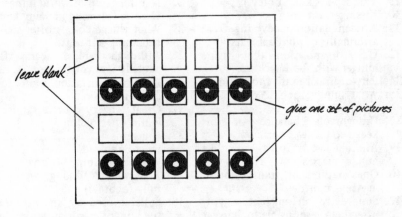

Created by Brethren House Ministries, 6301 56 Avenue N., St. Petersburg, Florida 33709. Used by permission.

68

PROCEDURE: For one player, stack the individual picture cards in front of the player and ask the child to match them with those glued on the board. To increase learning, as each picture is matched, the child should be asked to tell you something about the picture—what is going on, why the people need help, etc.

For two players, make two game boards with five pictures each. Stack the ten cards face down between the players. Each in turn draws a picture. If it matches a picture on the player's board, it goes in the appropriate space. If it does not match, it goes face up beside the stack. Playing continues until one player has matched all his/her pictures. To increase learning, the player could describe something about that picture to the other player before claiming it. The second time a picture appears, the player must tell something different.

Answers to puzzle 25

69

27

Concentration

This game, adapted from an old favorite, requires participants to remember various hunger facts or remedies through concentrating on where they are located on a board.

PREPARE BEFOREHAND: Game board and playing cards. To make the board, use a large piece of posterboard or a piece of cloth. Mark it into 12 squares large enough to accommodate the playing cards (see illustration following).

For playing cards, find six pictures either of hungry persons or of relief agencies at work (for example, wells, medical clinics, food lines, literacy classes). Cut out the pictures and glue them onto pieces of posterboard or 3 x 5 cards, making them uniform in size. On each of six other identical cards, for *readers* write a phrase that describes one of the six pictures, or for *non-readers* glue either a duplicate picture or a similar picture depicting the same aspect of hunger or relief.

Example: For a literacy class, matching card might read "Learning to Read" or show someone else reading.

PROCEDURE: 1. Explain all the pictures and matching word (or picture) cards to be sure all are understood. Each player must remember which two cards in each set form a pair.

2. Mix the cards up, place them face down on the playing board.

3. Each player, in turn, looks at two cards and shows them to other players. If they are a pair, the player keeps them and takes another turn. If the two cards are not a pair, the player replaces them on the board in their original positions,

Created by Brethren House Ministries, 6301 56th Avenue N., St. Petersburg, Florida 33709. Used by permission.

face down. The point of the game is to remember where pictures and words are that match, and to collect as many pairs as possible.

GAME BOARD

28

File Folder Fun

Colored file folders can be used to let children create their own games to play or to share with others. These folders can spotlight possibilities for helping people in need, and can involve young Christians in considering and evaluating the work of agencies for relief of poverty.

PREPARATION BEFOREHAND: Create one file folder activity as described below to be sure you understand process and to give children a model.

MATERIALS NEEDED: Colored file folder for each participant, promotional literature from relief agencies or from church literature depicting relief work (or hunger situations), colored oak tagboard and construction paper, masking tape, scissors, rubber cement, colored marking pens, scraps of felt or flannel, rulers, acetate sheets, two-pronged paper fasteners.

PROCEDURE: Explain that each person is going to create his/her own game about hunger. For young children you will probably want all the folders to have the same theme (for instance, "(name of agency) HELPS US GIVE . . . "). For older children you might suggest several themes from which they can choose (for example, "HUNGER FEELS LIKE . . . " "HUNGER LOOKS LIKE . . . ," "WE FIGHT HUNGER WITH . . . "). Give these directions:

1. At the top of the open folder, write the title of your game.

2. Make a pocket at the botton right-hand side of the folder to hold oak tagboard strips with printed words. (Suggested size for pocket: 8 cm. x 5 cm.) Tape the pocket on three sides with masking tape.

3. Select 4-6 small pictures that show something about your theme. For an agency, for instance, you might use one of a hand holding a cup of milk, a baby being examined in a clinic, fresh water

Created by Brethren House Ministries, 6301 56th Avenue N., St. Petersburg, Florida 33709. Used by permission.

72

coming from a new pump, etc. Cut the pictures neatly and glue them inside the folder. (*Double-glue* the pictures to insure permanent sticking. To double-glue, apply rubber cement to both surfaces to be joined, then allow them to *dry* completely before sticking them together firmly.)

Ask the "artists" to be as creative as possible in picture placement, but be sure to leave lots of space around them for word placement, other activities, and attractiveness.

4. Underneath each picture, glue colored construction paper. On top of the paper, glue a strip of felt or flannel.

5. Make word strips telling what the pictures show. (For pictures described above, you might write MILK, MEDICINE, CLEAN WATER). The strips should be approximately 2 cm. x 8 cm. to fit into the pocket and show when standing up. On the back of each strip, glue another strip of felt. When participants use the folder to consider what an agency does, they can stick the proper words under appropriate pictures.

6. Write these instructions on your pocket: "Match the words in this pocket with the pictures." Decorate the outside of folders as you wish.

You might want to suggest that participants create something with posterboard that can be manipulated—a spinner, a strip of posterboard to lift, plastic-covered maps for marking with water-soluble pens, etc. This encourages more participation and use of folders.

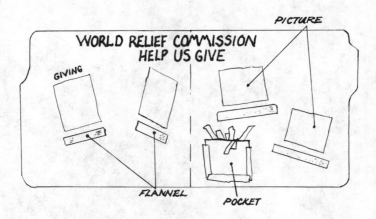

lifestyle evaluations

Christ came to offer us the abundant life; instead, most of us are trapped by the consumptive life. Yet our very habits of consumption are part of what keeps hungry people hungry.

The two evaluations and the skit in this section are designed to help participants ask themselves, "What do I really need? What do I have—possessions, habits, attitudes—that I can well do without?" Then, hopefully, we can begin to move prayerfully toward following an old New England proverb:

Use it up,

Wear it out,

Make it do, or

Do without!

Contents

Number	Game	Type	Time*
29	I Need, I Want, I Have . . .	Survey	20
30	Energy Consumption Inventory	Survey	10-15
31	What They See Is What They Get	Drama	20-30

* In minutes (approximate)

29

I Need, I Want, I Have . . .

PREPARE BEFOREHAND: Sheets similar to the sample below, one for each participant.

MATERIALS NEEDED: Survey sheets, pencils.

PROCEDURE: Let individuals complete their own surveys, then in groups of 4-5, discuss. What kinds of excess did they discover? What would they like to do with the excess? What steps can help prevent such excess from accumulating again? How can they dispose of the excess in such a way that others actually benefit? (Might suggest Goodwill, garage sales with benefits going to hunger, etc.)

SURVEY SHEET SAMPLE (add items of your own)

I Need, I Want, I Have

According to your own definition of "Need" & "Want" and your best account of "Have," complete the survey below by indicating how many you need, want, and have of each item.

N W H

____ ____ ____ 1. Shirts

____ ____ ____ 2. Pairs of shoes

____ ____ ____ 3. Hairdryers

____ ____ ____ 4. Car(s)

____ ____ ____ 5. Meals/day w/meat

____ ____ ____ 6. Televisions

____ ____ ____ 7. Friends

____ ____ ____ 8. Meals a day

____ ____ ____ 9. Bluejeans

____ ____ ____ 10. Books

____ ____ ____ 11. Records

VARIATION:

Instead of evaluating the number of possessions, evaluate quality of life, using a survey sheet similar to the one below:

I Need, I Want, I Have . . .

According to your own definition of "needs" and "wants," check the following (KEY: N = need, W = want). If you think you have what is listed check H for have.

N   W   H

_____ _____ _____ 1. The capacity to receive love
_____ _____ _____ 2. An electric hairdryer
_____ _____ _____ 3. More than 5 shirts
_____ _____ _____ 4. A job
_____ _____ _____ 5. Fulfillment in work
_____ _____ _____ 6. Underarm spray deodorant
_____ _____ _____ 7. A car
_____ _____ _____ 8. A tennis racket
_____ _____ _____ 9. Acceptance by others
_____ _____ _____ 10. Meat every meal
_____ _____ _____ 11. Make-up
_____ _____ _____ 12. The capacity to love
_____ _____ _____ 13. Time to relax
_____ _____ _____ 14. More than one T.V.
_____ _____ _____ 15. Air conditioning
_____ _____ _____ 16. 10 prs. of sock, hose
_____ _____ _____ 17. Realization of God's love
_____ _____ _____ 18. More than 4 shoes
_____ _____ _____ 19. Praise from friends
_____ _____ _____ 20. Indoor plumbing
_____ _____ _____ 21. Ability to read
_____ _____ _____ 22. Electricity
_____ _____ _____ 23. Haircuts
_____ _____ _____ 24. Bluejeans
_____ _____ _____ 25. A chance to cry
_____ _____ _____ 26. A college degree
_____ _____ _____ 27. 5 or more records
_____ _____ _____ 28. 3 meals a day (offered)
_____ _____ _____ 29. A church home
_____ _____ _____ 30. A private room
_____ _____ _____ 31. 5 underwear changes
_____ _____ _____ 32. More than 1 Bible

30

Type: Inventory
Time: 10-15 minutes

Energy Consumption Inventory

This inventory is designed to help participants consider personal habits of energy use, and begin asking how they can cut back on energy to free it for others in the world. During discussion, remember one thing: *no one rule applies to everybody or every family*. One person's luxury may be another's necessity. Any decisions made must take into account four factors:

cost (both to produce and to use)

personal preference, needs

time, saved or used

effect on total environment

MATERIALS NEEDED: pencils and paper for each participant.

PROCEDURE: 1. Let each participant privately list 15 items s/he uses frequently at home or work that use energy or for which energy was used in their production. (Remember that plastics are made from petroleum.)

2. Check 5 you could do without, without any sacrifice of your quality of life. Discuss in small groups (4-5).

3. Check 5 more you could do without, but which entail considerable change in lifestyle. In small groups discuss and suggest alternatives or substitutes.

31

Type: Drama
Time: 20-30 minutes

What They See Is What They Get

CHARACTERS: Helen Adams   Arlene Fisher
Bill Adams   Susie Fisher (10-12)
Caroline Adams (10-12)   Two poster bearers
Tim Adams (15-16)

SCENE: The Adams' living room. Need three chairs and a television (or a box painted to look like a television).

PROPS: Susie needs a book, Helen needs a legal pad, Bill needs a newspaper. You also need two posters, lettered large enough to be easily read from the audience. One reads "THEIR SITUATION IS DIFFERENT" and the other reads "THEY ARE DIFFERENT."

(Helen and Bill Adams sit facing the audience. He is reading a paper and she is working over a list on the legal pad. Caroline sprawls on the floor pretending to read a book, but actually watching television. She keeps her attention on the television even when speaking to her parents.)

BILL: Well, they've done it again.

HELEN: What, dear?

BILL: Raised taxes to increase welfare payments. I have nothing against helping people, but I hate paying taxes so deadbeats can loaf.

HELEN: Why, Bill Adams, that isn't so. Most people on welfare are children, mothers who can't leave the children, or over sixty-five. In this state hardly one person receives welfare who could be working.

BILL: Where'd you learn all that?

HELEN: From working in the church's self-help shop. We volunteers were given a tour of the part of town we're helping, and some stuff to read. I was really startled. Did you know there are people in town who are actually *hungry?*

BILL: Don't they get Food Stamps?

79

HELEN: Some of them. But there's a waiting period, then they get disqualified for all sorts of reasons—moving, a child graduating from school or getting a job—and have to wait again to requalify. Then some folks are too proud to accept the stamps, but go hungry. And those who do get them get only enough for the bare necessities—the cheapest cuts of meat and canned goods.

BILL: Seems to me like they shouldn't complain if it's free. Speaking of food, what's for supper?

HELEN: Liver.

CAROLINE: Yuck! I hate liver.

HELEN: Don't worry, dear, I have a hamburger for you.

CAROLINE: *(Casually.)* If we were poor, would I have to eat liver as a punishment?

HELEN: Punishment for what?

CAROLINE: For being poor. Daddy said you shouldn't complain if you get it free. That sounds like he thinks poor people ought to have to suffer.

BILL: That's not what I meant. I just think they ought to be grateful, like we are when we get a gift.

CAROLINE: Like when you say "Thank you" to Mrs. Jeffers every Christmas for those awful preserves she sends?

BILL: Yes, something like that.

CAROLINE: But we don't eat the preserves. Mother throws them out. Why should the poor people have to eat stuff they hate—is it different because they're poor?

BILL: I don't want to discuss it any further, Caroline. You'll understand when you're older. *(He retreats into his paper. Caroline shrugs and returns to the television.)*

(Enter two poster bearers, carrying posters so all can read them. Exit.)

HELEN: *(Musingly.)* You know, I talked to one woman in the self-help shop today. She's really strange—had a funny system of values.

BILL: *(Looks up from paper.)* Who's that, dear?

HELEN: A woman who came into the shop today. Arlene Fisher.

80

CAROLINE: Does she live on Wooten Street and have four children?

HELEN: I don't know. Why?

CAROLINE: There's a girl named Susie Fisher in my class. We took them a Christmas basket last year, remember? I had to take two cans, and you sent that soup we'd bought and didn't like. And when we got to Susie's, they didn't have a thing to eat in the house except a little bag of potato chips.

BILL: See what I mean? Potato chips—and nothing else. Wonder why the mother would buy potato chips instead of milk?

CAROLINE: Oh, Susie bought them. Me and Karen . . .

HELEN: Karen and I.

CAROLINE: Okay, Karen and I were buying them and I guess Susie didn't want to be different. But at lunchtime, that's all she had. We had our lunches. *(Virtuously.)* I shared my sandwich with her.

HELEN: That was nice of you, dear, but you need your food. You must tell Susie to use her money to buy lunch, and not junk.

CAROLINE: I'll tell her, but maybe she won't like the idea.

HELEN: She's probably learned from her mother. The woman in the shop today seems to buy the extras and not the necessities.

(Knock at the door. Helen answers it, returns followed by Arlene and Susie. Arlene is dressed very stylishly, but cheaply. Susie looks unkempt.)

HELEN: Why, Mrs. Fisher, I was just telling my husband you were in the shop today. Bill, this is Mrs. Fisher. Mrs. Fisher, Bill Adams.

BILL and ARLENE: How do you do?

HELEN: Susie, you're in class with Caroline, aren't you? You girls watch television while we talk.

SUSIE: Wow! A color TV! I want us to get us one of those things! *(Plops down beside Caroline and they are glued to the television.)*

81

HELEN: Mrs. Fisher, please sit down. (*They both sit.*) What can we do for you?

ARLENE: Mrs. Adams, I come for a special reason. I wouldn't barge in like this, but it's awful important.

HELEN: Yes?

ARLENE: My boy Junior is having a birthday next week, and he wants a bicycle real bad. I can't pay for it all at once, of course, so I wanted to get it on credit. But when I went to the store, they said I can't get credit because I never *had* credit. I can't get it, that is, unless somebody with credit signs with me. *(Anxiously.)* You have credit, don't you?

HELEN: Well, yes, but . . .

BILL: Mrs. Fisher, I'm afraid we can't sign just like that. If you weren't able to pay, we'd be liable for your bill. We barely make our own payments. I'm sure you understand.

ARLENE: I pay my bills. But I couldn't seem to save enough out of my Social Security check—I lost my husband, you know—to buy that bicycle on time. And Junior has his heart set on a new bike.

BILL: Perhaps we can help you find a second-hand bike.

ARLENE: *(With dignity.)* My Junior ain't going to have nobody's cast-off bike. It's his birthday, and I want him to have something real nice.

BILL: I don't mean a worn out one. The police have a sale of bikes they've picked up and nobody has claimed. Our son Tim got one there last month, and it's almost like new.

ARLENE: *(Brightens.)* Your son got a second-hand bike? Tim Adams? Wait until I tell Junior. Imagine that! He set his heart on a bike because Tim Adams got one, and now I find out his is secondhand. Can you tell me where to go?

BILL: *(Writes address on piece of newspaper, tears it off for her.)* Tell them I sent you. They should be pretty reasonable.

ARLENE: Thanks so much. Come on, Susie, we gotta go.

82

SUSIE: Aw, Ma, let me just finish this show. *(Her mother pulls her arm, she gets up protesting.)* Darn, I wish we had a color TV. Can we get one, Ma? I'll mind the baby all the time if you'll get me a color TV.

ARLENE: We'll see. *(To Helen.)* Honestly, there's no end to their wants, is there? *(Exits, with Susie in tow.)*

BILL: A color TV! And she can't even feed her family. Where do those people get values like that?

CAROLINE: Susie got hers from us.

HELEN: Caroline!

(Enter poster bearers, walk across stage with posters for all to see. (Exit.)

BILL: Caroline, go find Tim. I want to talk to him. *(Caroline reluctantly gets up and exits.)*

HELEN: Bill, was Mrs. Fisher right about not being able to get credit?

BILL: I suspect so, dear. She couldn't get it at our store.

HELEN: Why on earth not?

BILL: She's a poor credit risk. Her only source of income is Social Security, and she's got four children to feed. How do we know she'd pay? We just can't take the chance.

HELEN: I can't imagine living without credit. Why, it almost seems like we were born with it.

BILL: You *were* born a better credit risk. And I have a good job, so we get credit fairly easily. People like Mrs. Fisher don't have any money for luxury spending anyway. They don't need credit.

HELEN: But we don't use our credit for luxuries. I use it for gas, clothes, medicines—especially we use it when school begins, or at Christmas. I don't think we could make it without credit.

BILL: Yeah, but we pay our bills.

HELEN: Nobody knows if Mrs. Fisher would pay hers or not— nobody gives her a chance. Besides, we couldn't pay all *our* bills if we didn't have credit. Not every month, anyway.

BILL: Helen, don't worry about it. You just don't understand the business point of view. Mrs. Fisher is not the same as us, not at all.

(Enter poster bearers again, cross stage, exit.)

(Enter Tim and Caroline. Tim crosses to stand in front of Bill.)

TIM: You wanted to see me, Dad?

BILL: Yes, son. I had a call from Mr. Williams at your school today. He said you decided not to run for class president. Why's that?

TIM: Aw, Dad, It's not that big a thing.

BILL: No—I want to know why. What he said didn't make sense—that you felt there were better ways to spend money? What money?

TIM: Well, things are expected of the class president. You have to wear sharp clothes and take out sharp girls to expensive places. I just don't want to get into that.

BILL: Why not? We dress you well enough, don't we? Even if you do prefer most of the time to look like a tramp. And if you want to take out girls, we'll take care of that, too. What's the problem?

TIM: *(Shuffles around, then sits down and leans toward his father.)* Well, it started in Sunday School. We had a unit on values, and when we listed ours they looked pretty trivial. Dressing right and living in the right neighborhood—that sort of thing. Why, when I told them I got a second-hand bike at the Police Station, some guys acted like I'd got it from Mars. Second hand wasn't in their vocabulary. But then I got to thinking about stewardship.

BILL: Yeah? Go on.

TIM: You know, in the Bible where it says not to worry about where you will get food or clothes? Well, it seems to me that we spend an awful lot of time thinking about those things.

HELEN: Tim Adams, you never worried about a meal in your life.

84

TIM: No, but *you* spend a lot of time working to give us the best clothes and the best food. I think we spend too much on those things.

HELEN: You can say that again. After this month's Master Charge bill we are all going on an immediate austerity campaign.

CAROLINE: *(Carefully.)* What's an austerity campaign?

TIM: *(Sarcastic.)* That's where you pretend you're poor, but you aren't. Then when you get tired of it, you go back to normal.

CAROLINE: Will I have to wear my oldest clothes? Or can I wear my new outfit to the class party?

HELEN: Of course you can wear your new outfit to the party, Dear. We want you to look nice, after all.

CAROLINE: I think I understand. We'll wear our old clothes when we want to think about the bills, and our good ones when we want to look nice?

TIM: You've got it, kid.

BILL: I still don't see what all this has to do with being class president. Couldn't you be president, and just be different?

TIM: *(Thoughtfully.)* You mean, set a new pattern? Dress like I wanted to and date who I wanted?

CAROLINE: Yeah. No sharp girls would go out with *you* anyhow.

BILL: Caroline! *(She makes a face, returns to television watching.)* Tim, I think you have something there. Maybe you could show what difference being a Christian makes in being class president.

TIM: I'll think about it, Dad. *(Notices the television.)* Hey! It's time for Star Trek. Caroline, change channels.

CAROLINE: No. Mother said I could watch this program.

HELEN: Oh, dear, yes I did. Sorry, Tim, I forgot about your show.

TIM: It's not fair. Everytime I want to watch a show, she's got the TV.

BILL: Maybe we need to get you kids each a little TV for your rooms. Then I could see the news in peace.

CAROLINE: Well, so much for the austerity campaign. We're just like the Fishers, buying a TV when we can't afford one.

HELEN: You know, Caroline's right. Except I wonder if she's got it backwards. Maybe the Fishers are just like us. And maybe we all need to think about our value systems. Does being a Christian have anything to say about what we buy, and how much? Look at our bills. New clothes when we had good ones in the closet. Sports equipment for Tim when he can use all he needs at school. A sleeping bag for Caroline's slumber parties, when a quilt would do. A weekly hairdresser for me.

CAROLINE: Mrs. Fisher goes to the hairdresser, too. Her hair looked like yours used to.

HELEN: Yes, her beauty parlor is probably one style behind. I wonder how much we middle-class Christians set the styles for the rest of the world. If we wear new clothes, so does Mrs. Fisher.

CAROLINE: She sure looked sharp.

HELEN: Yes, but her clothes weren't well made. They'll wear out in a few washings. She could get better things at the self-help shop, but she doesn't like second-hand.

CAROLINE: She's getting a second-hand bike because Tim did.

HELEN: Yes, she is. Maybe if I bought some things from the shop as well as taking things down, she'd see it's all right to wear recycled clothes. Now about these bills. New golf clubs for you, Bill, and lots of golf balls. I didn't realize they were so costly.

BILL: Tom Waters buys his from kids around the course. Wonder why I always thought I needed new ones? In fact, Tom and I could really share clubs. He plays on Tuesdays, and I play on Thursdays. Wonder why we never thought of that before. We're always discussing the rising costs of living.

HELEN: There are probably lots of ways we could share if we

86

thought about it. Washers and dryers, vacuum cleaners, tents . . .

CAROLINE: *(To Tim.)* How about that. Adults talking about sharing *their* toys for a change!

TIM: Hush. They're really onto something.

BILL: You know, this really grabs me. The very things we criticize the Fishers for—wanting new instead of recycled things, buying extras instead of essentials—those are the very things they see us doing. How are they to know we bought essentials first?

HELEN: Then maybe we'd better set a better example.

CAROLINE: Well . . . I guess that means I stop buying junk with my lunch money, hun? But what're we going to do with all the money we save?

TIM: Our youth group is saving money for a hunger offering. Maybe we could do that as a family. Wow! This will blow the group's mind. A whole family trying to live up to Christian principles!

BILL: Hey, don't get too full of yourself yet. We're not going to get instant halos. But maybe we can begin to think a bit about what's really important and what isn't.

CAROLINE: I just want to know one thing. Will this austerity campaign last very long?

HELEN: Honey, I don't think this is going to be an austerity campaign. I think it may very well be a completely different way of living.

87

songs

Singing together can loosen up a group before a serious program and also teach hunger facts. Similarly, during worship new songs or new words to old tunes can express concern and make us more aware of hunger. The songs in this section might inspire your local poets to compose their own! Each song gives one or more facts about hunger or illustrates one area of Christian concern.

Contents

32

Feed My Sheep

Words & Music by Mary Shinholser

Je-sus said, "Feed my sheep, dry the tears of
Je-sus said, "Feed my lambs, in this world you

those who weep, If you do this lov-ing-ly, you've
are my hands, Bear the bur-den will-ing-ly, and

done it un-to me —" So feed the hun-gry,
do it all for me —"

clothe the poor; give the wear-y rest — And if we

bring them in in Je-sus' name, then

He will be our guest.

© Copyright 1976 by Mary Shinholser   Used by permission of the composer

33

Two Fish, Five Loaves

*Dedicated to Marge Luce
and to the Genesis Singers*

RICHARD AVERY
DONALD MARSH

One lit-tle boy a long time a—go had two fish.
How ma-ny fish and how ma-ny loaves have you got?

One lit-tle boy a long time a—go had five loaves.
How ma-ny fish and how ma-ny loaves have you got?

Well, he off-ered them up to five thou-sand sup—per hung-ry
Are you will-ing to share or stor-ing up care--ful-ly a-

peo-ple on the shore And when they were done i-
gainst some rain-y day? In Jes--us---'s plan you

ma-gine the fun they had col-lect-ing twelve bask-ets more.
get a bo-nan-----za when you give what you have a---way.

End the song with the first 2 phrases of the 2nd stanza, repeated over and over.

© Copyright 1976 by Richard K. Avery and Donald S. Marsh
From BOOK #7. Used by permission
Proclamation Products, Inc., Port Jervis, NY 12771

91

34

Walk Tall In The Noonday Sun

Words & Music by Mary Shinholser

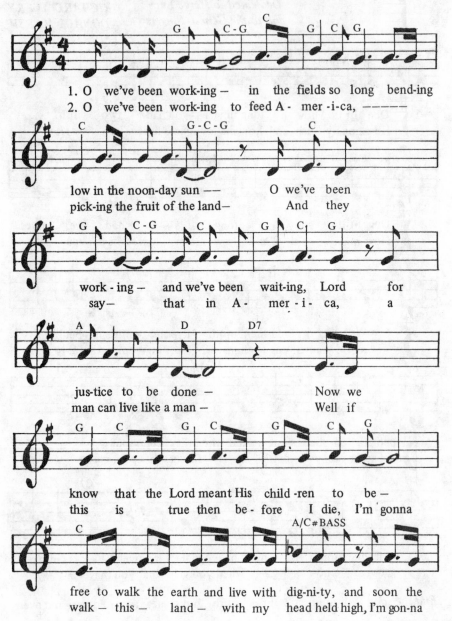

1. O we've been work-ing — in the fields so long bend-ing
2. O we've been work-ing to feed A-mer-i-ca, ———

low in the noon-day sun — O we've been
pick-ing the fruit of the land— And they

work-ing — and we've been wait-ing, Lord for
say— that in A-mer-i-ca, a

jus-tice to be done — Now we
man can live like a man — Well if

know that the Lord meant His child-ren to be —
this is true then be-fore I die, I'm gonna

free to walk the earth and live with dig-ni-ty, and soon the
walk — this — land — with my head held high, I'm gon-na

92

Dedicated to America's Migrant Farm Workers

day will come— when you and me will walk
reach out my hands— and touch the sky and walk

tall in the noon-day sun — chorus. Walk
tall in the noon-day sun —

tall broth-ers and sis — ters — For

jus-tice will be done — Walk

tall sis -ters and bro — thers, Walk

tall in the noon-day sun ——————.

© Copyright 1976 by Mary Shinholser   Used by permission of the composer

93

35

Whate'er You Do

by Marion Lucciola and Patti Sprinkle

Tune: Faith of Our Fathers

1. When I was hungry, you offered me food,
   When I was thirsty, you gave me drink,
   When I was stranger, you opened your door,
   When I was naked, your coat I wore.

Chorus: Whate'er you do to the least of these,
   What you have done, you've done to me.

2. I was imprisoned, you came to my cell,
   Stood by my bedside when I lay ill,
   Though I disguised it, you still knew my face,
   Now come, oh bless-ed, claim your right place!

36

We Plough the Fields with Tractors

(Author unknown)

(Tune: "We Plough the fields and scatter . . . ")

1. We plough the fields with tractors,
   with drills we sow the land,
   but growth is still the wondrous gift
   of God's almighty hand.
   We add our fertilizers
   to help the growing grain—
   but for its full fruition
   it needs God's sun and rain.

Refrain: All good gifts around us are sent from heaven above;
Then thank the Lord, O thank the Lord for all his love.

2. With many new machines now
   we do the work each day;
   we reap the fields with combines
   we bale the new-mown hay,
   but it is God who gives us
   inventive skills and drives
   which lighten labor's drudgery
   and give us fuller lives.

3. Then why are people starving
   when we have life so good?
   Why, then, in cities' garbage
   must some still search for food?
   Because we've been too selfish
   to share what God has given,
   therefore life is for millions
   more like a hell than heaven.

37

How Much Is Enough?

(a song for children)

1. How much is e - nough? How man - y times a day must we   eat?
2. How much is e - nough? How man - y kinds of food do we need?
3. How much is e - nough? How man - y pairs of shoes do we need?
4. How much is e - nough? Just how man - y rooms do we   need?
5. How much is e - nough? Just how man - y toys do we need?
6. Can I do with - out some toys and clothes and snacks ev - ery day?

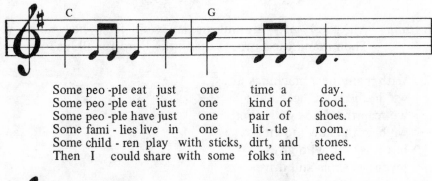

Some peo -ple eat just   one   time a   day.
Some peo -ple eat just   one   kind of   food.
Some peo -ple have just   one   pair of   shoes.
Some fami - lies live in   one   lit - tle room.
Some child - ren play with sticks, dirt, and stones.
Then I   could share with some   folks in   need.

How   man - y times a   day   must we   eat?
How   man - y kinds of food do we   need?
How   man - y pairs of shoes do we   need?
Just   how   man - y rooms do we   need?
Just   how   man - y toys do we   need?
Can   I   do with - out just to   share?

96

38

Type: Song for Fun Together

One Little, Two Little

(Tune: "One Little, Two Little, Three Little Indians")

One Little, two little, three senior citizens
Arrested daily in Miami
They were merely combating inflation
They were shoplifting food—ugh!*

39

Type: Song for Fun Together

If All the World Were Changed

(Tune: "The More We Get Together")

Chorus: If all the world were changed into a little village,
A funny little village this whole world would be.

Verses: Half of the village would always be hungry
While six percent were eating in complacency.

One-fourth were starving and ten percent dying,
While six percent consumed one-third the energy.

And those six percent would have three-fourths the
grain store,
With half a hungry village there for all to see.

Final Chorus: If all the world were changed into a little village,
A painful little village this old world would be.*

---

*Facts for these songs documented in Bread for the World sheet #9-1, "Some Facts and Statistics Related to World Hunger."

longer
simulations

The five games in this section are all designed to take up to one hour to play. Before using any of them, read carefully the pages entitled "Before You Play These Games . . ." and become thoroughly familiar with the game you plan to use. Each game demonstrates to players the relationship between the world's "haves" and "have nots." The games are somewhat similar, but each has a particular thrust that warrants including it in this anthology.

Contents

Number	Game	Type	Time*
40	Before You Play Any of These Games . . .		
41	World Food Crisis Simulation	Simulation	60
42	Seeing It as It Is	Simulation	30-45
43	The Poverty Game	Simulation	30 +
44	Road to a Well-fed Village	Simulation	Open
45	Fastathon	Simulation	Open
46	Hunger	Simulation	45-60

* In minutes (approximate)

40

Before You Play Any of These Games...

These next two chapters contain longer simulations and food experiences that teach something about the world hunger situation.

Before you use any of them with a group, here are a few **THINGS TO DO, THINK ABOUT AND WATCH OUT FOR.***

GETTING THE BACKGROUND:

Accept that there are different kinds of learning and things to learn. Games are not designed to teach names and dates or content; rather they teach concepts, strategic thinking, communication skills, descision-making, conflict resolution, bargaining, need to compromise, etc.

Be prepared for a different role: that of facilitator and fellow inquirer—not authority figure.

Expect some confusion, loose ends, improvisation, and noise.

PLAYING THE GAME:

Keep instructions brief. Let participants discover strategies. Do not worry about whether participants have learned every rule, lest interest wane. Some rules can be learned in course of play.

Don't hover and coach. Let participants make mistakes and profit from them.

Be prepared to improvise, for something may go wrong or the unexpected may happen.

---

* From *Hunger on Spaceship Earth Simulation Game,* produced by the World Hunger Project, New York Metropolitan Regional Office of the American Friends Service Committee, 15 Rutherford Place, New York, NY 10003. Used by permission.

DEBRIEFING AND FOLLOW-UP:

Debriefing is essential; indeed, failure to debrief adequately may leave participants with a distorted view of what was simulated.

What happened in the game? What were the goals? What strategies were effective in accomplishing those goals? Which had negative results?

Can you recall your feelings during the game? What were they? What was happening at the time?

What actions led to what results? What cause and effect relationship came out of the playing?

What would have happened if the rules or values had been changed?

How did the game compare with reality? What additional factors would have made the game more realistic? How could the game be redesigned to be more realistic? (The discussion of the real world may require considerable follow-up study.)

Did what happened in the game seem fair? Was this the fault of the game or the real world?

What hypotheses about reality did the game suggest? What needs to be done to confirm these hypotheses?

41

World Food Crisis Simulation

By Tim Hetrich

PURPOSE:

This simulation was designed to show the predicament of the under-developed areas of the world which can't afford to buy food from the few food exporting countries.

PREPARE BEFOREHAND: Trading cards (one-half of 3 x 5 cards work well) labeled: Tea, Oil, Teak, Bamboo, Jade, Diamonds, Zinc, Cocoa, Skins, Coffee, Rubber, Copper, Clothes, Wines, Watches, Money, Machinery/Equipment. You will need about 10 of each of these.

MATERIALS NEEDED: Trading cards prepared ahead, 3 dozen soft cookies. You might also have name tags and markers so each "Continent" can label its citizens.

PROCEDURE:

1. Divide into five world areas.

   North America in this game represents the world food producing area. *Europe* is an industrial power that does not have an abundance of food. *Africa, Southeast Asia,* and *Latin America* cannot produce enough food to sustain their populations.

   Each participant should choose the area of his/her choice until each area has reached its designated population.

   If 20 play:

N. America	– 2 people	L. America	– 4 people
Europe	– 3 people	SE Asia	– 6 people
		Africa	– 5 people

Originally printed by the Pennsylvania Southeast Conference, United Church of Christ, 620 Main Street, Box G, Collegeville, PA. 19426. Used by permission.

If 100 play:

N. America	– 10 people	L. America	– 20 people
Europe	– 15 people	SE Asia	– 30 people
		Africa	– 25 people

2. Go over the purpose and directions for the game with the group. Clue North Americans in that they should go for the best trades, not use their consciences in trading.

DIRECTIONS: Each team (world area) will be given cookies which combined represent the amount of food available in the world. Each team will also be given trading cards representing products which they can trade with one another or sell for pieces of cookie. (North America will be given no products, only cookies.) During each round of 10 minutes, participants are to trade products for enough cookies to keep their populations alive. *1½ cookies per team is the bare minimum of food needed to keep the population alive for a year.* Each of the 3 rounds represents one year.

3. Distribute cookies and trading cards as follows:

North America	4 cookies	No products*
Europe	2 cookies	Clothes, Wines, Watches, Machinery/Equipment
Southeast Asia	1 cookie	Tea, Oil, Teak, Bamboo, Jade
Africa	1 cookie	Diamonds, Zinc, Cocoa, Skins
Latin America	1 cookie	Coffee, Oil, Rubber, Copper

4. *ROUND ONE*

Before trading begins, notify the three poorer areas that each has had a disaster. In *Southeast Asia,* a drought; in *Latin America,* government instability has interfered with national food production and services; in *Africa,* poor planning has caused a poor harvest. Take a small piece of each of their cookies.

Ask each group (if groups are large) to choose 2-3 spokespersons to do the trading for the whole team, consulting with the team before making major trades.

Permit 10 minutes for trading to occur.

---

* This is the only unrealistic part of this game, for in actual fact North America produces fertilizers, equipment, and tools which undeveloped nations need and must buy. (Editor's note.)

103

After time is called, have each group report back to the leader. On the basis of that report, the leader should post a report of how many people will survive that year from each group:

If a group has 1 cookie, 10% of the people will die.

If a group has ¾ cookie, 20% will die.

If a group has ½ cookie, 30% will die.

Eat the remaining cookies.

5. *ROUND TWO*

Give out new cookies as before.

Again natural disasters have struck the poorer areas of the world: *SE Asia,* monsoons have destroyed tons of food; *Africa,* drought ruined thousands of acres of otherwise good farmland; *Latin America,* poor storing facilities, poor food transportation, and animal raids on food destroyed tons of food. Take ¼ cookie from each.

Permit 10 minutes for trading to occur.

Again report back and post population survival statistics. Eat remaining cookies.

6. *ROUND THREE*

Give out new cookies.

This was a good growing year, with no major disasters. Permit 10 minutes for trading to occur.

Report back and post population survival statistics. Eat remaining cookies.

7. *End of Simulation*

Call the group together to talk it out, especially feelings. Use such questions as:

What were your feelings about the game? What did it bring out?

How did the underdeveloped areas feel when they couldn't get enough food to support their people?

Did you see an effort developing to solve the food crisis? How did it come about?

What can the Church do?

This simulation was developed by Tim Hetrich, while he was still in high school, for the Pennsylvania Southeast Conference of the

United Church of Christ. Tim, later a student at the University of Pittsburgh and a member of the World Food Crisis Task Force of the Pennsylvania Southeast Conference of the U.C.C., has this to say about his game:

The purpose of this simulation when I first began to develop it was to experience, in some small way, how people in poorer areas of the world feel when they know some people have an abundance of food as they starve.

"Why won't they share when they have so much?" "They always seem to have enough grain to sell to other nations at pretty high prices."

Some of these same thoughts and questions may have crossed your mind as you played this simulation, along with a small portion of the feelings of discouragement and even disgust which many people in third world nations feel daily.

If this has happened, the experience was of some help in getting us inside the world food crisis, and hopefully from there to some real action in support of conquering this devastating problem for the sake of humankind and for the glory of God.

42

Seeing It as It Is

PURPOSE:

This simulation is designed to visualize the difference in income between eight nations of the world, using trade as one possible way of narrowing the gap between them.

PREPARATION BEFOREHAND:

For each 8 players prepare cards as shown below. (For a very large group, you might have 8 players actually play the game while others observe.)

MATERIALS NEEDED:

Playing cards prepared beforehand. One dollar *in pennies* for each eight players. Tables at which to play.

PROCEDURE:

1. Divide the group into tables of 8 players each. Give each person at the table a card and ask him/her to read aloud what is on that card to identify him/herself to the whole table.

2. Distribute pennies to each player according to the percent of group income indicated on the card (2% = 2¢, 25% = 25¢).

3. Instruct players that for 10 minutes they are to trade with one another for products. The idea is to increase their countries' dollar holdings (represented by the pennies) in the world market. (If one table plays and the rest of the group observes, players should speak loudly and clearly.)

4. When time is called, discuss players' reactions with such questions as:

   How did you feel when you saw your percent of group income?
   When you got your pennies?

What did you think of trading practices you participated in? Those you observed?

What did you learn about world trade from this game? What do you think might improve the world trade situation?

Playing Cards* (Prepare one set for each table)

Name of Country: INDIA
 	
Population   494.6 million
Per Capita Income $88.00
Products: tea, fibers,
    cashew nuts
Percent of Group
    Income   2
	Name of Country: KOREA
	
	Population 28.6 million
	Per Capita Income $120.00
	Products: tungsten, silk, fish,
	    rice, agriculture
	Percent of Group
	    Income 2

Name of Country: GHANA
 	
Population   8.0 million
Per Capita Income $226.00
Products: cocoa, diamonds,
    manganese
Percent of Group
    Income   4
	Name of Country: BRAZIL
	
	Population 83.0 million
	Per Capita Income $224.00
	Products: coffee, cocoa,
	    cotton
	Percent of Group
	    Income 3

Name of Country: MEXICO
 	
Population   42.9 million
Per Capita Income $434.00
Products: cotton, metals,
    coffee
Percent of Group
    Income   8
	Name of Country: PORTUGAL
	
	Population 9.2 million
	Per Capita Income $367.00
	Products: agriculture, fish,
	    forestry
	Percent of Group
	    Income 4

Name of Country:
    UNITED STATES
 	
Population   196.0 million
Per Capita Income $3,240.00
Products: manufactured
    goods
Percent of Group
    Income   52
	Name of Country:
	    UNITED KINGDOM
	
	Population 54.0 million
	Per Capita Income $1550.00
	Products: manufactured
	    goods
	Percent of Group
	    Income 25

* Facts from Barbara Ward's *Lopsided World* (N.Y.: Norton, 1968).

107

43

Type: Longer Simulation
Time: 30 minutes + discussion

The Poverty Game

by James Egbert

PURPOSE:

To show the dynamics of poverty in the midst of affluence.

PREPARATION BEFOREHAND:

This game requires a good bit of preparation and a good leader but it can be a lot of fun. Thoroughly familiarize yourself with it before time to play!

Make paper money out of construction paper in $\frac{1}{2}¢$, $1¢$, $2¢$, and $5¢$ denominations (use a different color for each). Place money in envelopes for "citizens" (see below) as follows:

For ten citizens:			*For twenty citizens:*		
1 envelope contains		17¢	1 envelope contains		20¢
1 "	"	12¢	1 "	"	15¢
1 "	"	10¢	1 "	"	12¢
2 "	"	6¢	2 "	"	10¢
2 "	"	3¢	4 "	"	6¢
3 "	"	nothing	4 "	"	3¢
			6 "	"	nothing

You also need money for storekeepers' change and money in $\frac{1}{2}¢$ pieces for the welfare worker(s).

Adapted by permission of the publisher from *Colloquy*, March 1969. Copyright 1969 by United Church Press.

Prepare nametags for the following players:

> police officer
>
> storekeeper(s) — in a large group, you may want to have three or four stores
>
> welfare worker(s)
>
> minister
>
> game supervisor
>
> organizer of the poor
>
> observer(s)

You might also include in each money envelope a colored badge for each "economic level" to wear to identify them to others.

MATERIALS NEEDED:

A collection of magazines, a quantity of white glue, scissors, packet of pipe cleaners, package of bright construction paper, assortment of dull faded construction paper, foil, straws, clean and dirty yarn, and anything else that can be used in making collages. Also paper for collage backgrounds, markers and/or crayons, pencils.

Tables to work on and other tables for your "store(s)."
Envelopes containing money and colored badges; nametags.

PROCEDURE:

1. Explain to the whole group the purpose of the game. Divide the group into the following categories: citizens (the majority of your group), storekeeper(s), a police officer, a minister, welfare worker(s), organizer of the poor, group of observers, and a game supervisor (who is familiar with the rules—probably yourself).

2. Distribute nametags to appropriate persons and distribute envelopes to the citizens. Ask them not to open their envelopes until they have received instructions. Give the welfare worker half-cents to use for payments and storekeepers money for change.

3. Give each group the appropriate following instructions: (may be written on 3 x 5 cards). *Citizens* are told they must each produce

109

a collage in the allotted time (may be 10, 15, or 20 minutes). They can use the money in their sealed envelopes to purchase supplies at the store (s). Their name badges indicate which economic level they belong to. Explain that many citizens are poor, and some have no money at all. They may call on friends, welfare worker(s), and the minister, or get funds *any other way they can*. At the end of the time period, each citizen *must* have a collage to hang on the wall.

Storekeepers are told to sell materials the workers need. In a Glue Store, glue costs 1¢, in a Paper Store, a small sheet of colored tissue paper is 2¢, scissors cost 3¢, etc. Storekeepers may overcharge, sell damaged merchandise or bargain. They should encourage wealthy customers to spend money. The poor should be mistreated. Near the end of the time limit, they can reduce prices or increase them. They can also use the police officer to collect IOUs from customers, and citizens may be jailed for not paying.

The *police officer* patrols the area, spying on the poor and harassing them. Especially watch for cheating and stealing, and rough up offenders. Ridicule poor people and side with the wealthy. Make arrests and place offenders in "jail" for 1 to five minutes.

The *welfare worker (s)* has a few half-cent pieces to help the poor. Require them to fill out long forms and wait for long periods to get a little money. Ask personal questions like: "What will you do with your money? How much money did you get? Have you tried to get help somewhere else?"

The *minister* gives out very little money, which has been gotten by asking the wealthy for donations. Talk to the poor about their relationship to the church and give out money only to those who promise to attend church.

The *supervisor* directs the game. Know who is playing what role and who has money. Act as a catalyst by being very pushy and insulting. Demand that the poor produce better, but be unsatisfied with the work they do. May even reject some finished products, saying they could be better.

110

The *organizer of the poor* attempts to unite them. Organize sit-ins, demonstrations, boycotts, etc. May achieve goals either constructively or destructively. The police will, of course, oppose this activity.

Game observers need to make a list quickly of who has how much money, and who is playing what other role. Record comments and interaction between players for later discussion.

4. Begin the game. At the end of your allotted time period (10, 15, or 20 minutes) call time. Display all collages for cheers and jeers.

5. To begin discussion, ask for feelings from the players. Be sure to let the observers tell what they saw happening in terms of group dynamics. You might also use such questions as:

In what ways was this like real life?

In what ways was it *unlike* real life?

What insights did you get during this game?

In what ways is real life unfair to the poor? In what ways do we contribute to that unfairness? What can we do?

44

Road to a Well-fed Village

This game was initially developed by Bonnie Munson and the children at Brethren House in St. Petersburg, Florida. The purpose of the game is to experience the impact of certain factors on a whole village where people are hungry and poor. Participants are asked to design their own board game, then play it.

In congregational settings each family might design a game together to take home. A youth group might design games for elementary classes, or a table of participants might design a game for immediate use.

MATERIALS NEEDED:

Instructions, posterboard, markers or crayons, pens and pencils, list of Hunger Factors from below. (Instructions and Hunger Factors may be mimeographed or written on posters.)

ADDITIONAL MATERIALS NEEDED TO PLAY THE GAME:

Colored beans to use as markers, 3 pennies and a paper cup.

INSTRUCTIONS:

1. Pencil in on the game board a "road" at least 1½ inches wide and mark it off in squares large enough to write in. Your road may run around the outer edge of the board Monopoly-style, spiral in or wander. Go over it in marker. (For elementary groups, prepare the boards ahead of time so children can get on with creating the game.)
2. Label the first square "Hungry" and the last one "Well-fed."
3. Using Hunger Factors from the list below and your imagination, write directions on some of the squares, indicating how many spaces a player is to go ahead or back, and the cause. You might designate some squares "Wait One Turn" and others "Return to Hungry." Leave approximately ½ the squares blank. Be sure to have twice as many "Go back" squares as "Go ahead" ones!
4. You may want to decorate your board with markers or with pictures of food and hungry people.

SUGGESTED RULES FOR PLAY:

1. The player who ate least recently begins.
   Shake the 3 pennies in the paper cup and dump them on the

112

table. The number of heads showing determines how many spaces the player should move. Move the chosen bean to the appropriate square and follow any instructions as a part of that move.

2. Play clockwise around the table.
3. Whenever a player reaches "Well-fed," s/he then moves his or her bean back to join the player farthest back, and the two of them move together, using both players' throws to determine how far to move. When they both reach "Well-fed," they may choose whether to rest or to go back and join yet another player and help him/her.
4. *The game is not over until all players are well-fed!* Nobody wins unless everybody does—the opponent is not other players, but the disasters which threaten success.

HUNGER FACTORS

"Go-back" factors

drought
floods
seed was diseased
trucks of fertilizer didn't come
political revolution
poor harvest
population increased
epidemic killed able-bodied adults
landlord brought new car, rents up
war—sons drafted
war—fields bombed
poor transportation to market
rats got into storage bins
drought elsewhere—refugees came
had to borrow to buy seed
ox died
ads convinced you to buy baby
    formula
youths leave for urban ghettos
bridge out between you and market
local currency value down
worldwide good harvest—prices down

"Go ahead" factors

it finally rained
Christian friends sent seed
market prices up
good harvest
Christian friends sent a well
village co-op bought small
    tractor
reading classes begun in village
co-op got started for crops
agriculture school started
    nearby
epidemic killed elderly and
    children (population de-
    creased)
bought 2 sheep to start a
    clock
village got a doctor
educated youths return to
    village

113

45

Type: Longer Simulation
Time: Open

Fastathon

PURPOSE:

The Fastathon really serves three purposes:

(a) participants experience to some degree what hunger actually feels like, and begin to identify with hungry people;

(b) participants raise a good deal of money for hunger action;

(c) participants have a time and a place to become better educated about the problems of hunger.

This is one of the best methods around for accomplishing those three purposes. It is particularly good for youth groups, church school classes, and other self-contained groups.

PREPARATION BEFOREHAND: Print up Sponsor Sheets for each participant (see sample below). At least two weeks before the Fastathon each participant should receive a Sponsor Sheet to begin signing up sponsors. The Planning Committee should also decide on games, audio visuals, and the kind of closing meal they want, and line up materials, reserve films, and purchase groceries. Be sure to preview all films to be sure equipment is in running order. Publicity in the community is appropriate.

PROCEDURE: The length of a fastathon is up to the group, but 30 hours is suggested. Church Fellowship Halls make especially good places to meet—some groups bring sleeping bags and spend the night, others go home and meet again in the morning. Members either eat nothing, or merely drink water or fruit juices. During the fast, use time together for hunger education, and perhaps even to map out a strategy for hunger action together at a later date.

Sometimes also called Starvathon

114

Conclude your time tigether with some sort of symbolic meal: rice and tea, communion and worship, fruit and cheese, etc. Be sure that members collect from their sponsors. You may want to have a special time of dedication for money collected through the event.

Note: A special instruction pamphlet with a sponsor record included is available from CROP, P.O. Box 968, Elkhart, Indiana 46514.

Sample Sponsor Sheet

Name of Sponsor Address	Pledge per hour	Total Amount
1.		
2.		$
3.		
4.		
etc.		
TOTAL SPONSORS: TOTAL $		

46

Type: Longer simulation
Time: 45 - 60 minutes

Hunger

by Jim and Robin Farinet

PURPOSE:

To sharpen our sensitivity to the needs of the world.

PREPARATION BEFOREHAND:

Prepare 6 medium bags as shown below and 1 large bag (also shown). Label with marker and place on a table.

Also prepare 3 envelopes, labeled front and back, and enclose money.

label
front: FAMILY A   FAMILY B   FAMILY C

label
back: Contents: $4000.   Contents: $300.   Contents: $100.
        Set aside 75% for   Set aside 20% for   Set aside 10% for
        housing, clothing,   housing, clothing,   housing, clothing,
        education, defense,   education, defense,   education, defense,
        fun, taxes, etc.   fun, taxes, etc.   fun, taxes, etc.
        DO NOT DISCLOSE   DO NOT DISCLOSE   DO NOT DISCLOSE
        THIS INFORMATION.   THIS INFORMATION.   THIS INFORMATION.

Developed by Reverend Jim and Robin Farinet, Christ United Church of Christ, Orrville, Ohio. Originally published by the Office for Church Life and Leadership, United Church of Christ. Used by permission.

FAMILY A	FAMILY B	FAMILY C

enclose
money: $4,000 as follows: $300 as follows: $100 as follows:

	FAMILY A		FAMILY B		FAMILY C
7	$500-bills	2	$100-bills	3	$20-bills
3	$100-bills	3	$20-bills	4	$10-bills
8	$20-bills	4	$10-bills		
4	$10-bills				

PLAYERS:

This game is most effective when used with small groups of 10 to 15 people with a game leader for each group. The game leader conducts the simulation and acts as a discussion enabler. If more than one group plays simultaneously, one game leader serves as the general director.

MATERIALS NEEDED:

6 medium paper bags; 1 large paper bag; 3 plain envelopes; 1 marker; toy paper money (raid your Monopoly set):

7	$500 bills	14	$20 bills
5	$100 bills	12	$10 bills

PROCEDURE:

STATEMENT (BY GENERAL LEADER): *Because it is often difficult to relate to the overpowering statistics of the hunger situation, this game has been developed to sharpen our sensitivity to the needs of our world. As the game unfolds try to be aware of your feelings.*

1. Divide into groups of 10-15.

2. Divide each group into 3 teams, called families, with % rounded off for simplicity:

    20% of group = Family A   [Example: in a group of 12,
20%-30% of group = Family B   there would be 2 in Family A,
50%-60% of group = Family C   3 in Family B, 7 in Family C]

The percentages represent an approximation of the world population in each income bracket according to figures from CROP.

3. Give each family its envelope, instructing each family not to tell the other families how much money it has or what is on its envelope.

4. Families count the money and return the stated percentage to the envelope, holding the remaining food money in their hands. The tax collector (game leader) collects the envelopes.

5. Families take turns going to the market place (table) to buy food. Each family may purchase *one item* of food *at a time in turn:* first Family A, then Family B, then Family C. Continue in turn until no further purchases can be made. Game leaders should pay close attention to feelings and conversations in families for later discussion.

6. *Inform:*

FAMILY C—	FAMILY B—	FAMILY A—
1/3 must die. They have no choice; 1/3 have starved to death. They must choose (elderly, children, etc.) who will die. [Have the deceased separate themselves from the family.]	They have just enough food to subsist. They will be hungry, but will survive. (One may choose to die so others eat better, but they have a choice.)	Each has gained 10 pounds.

DISCUSSION:

1. The game leader asks Family C, then Family B, finally Family A, *"Were you satisfied with your purchase?"* Discuss feelings.

2. The game leader asks Family C, then Family B, finally Family A, *"How do you feel?"* Keep discussion brief.

   Typical responses: C—total frustration; sad about situation
   B—angry, resentful, even violent
   A—guilty

3. The game leader asks Family C, then Family B, finally Family A, *"What can you do about your situation?"*

   Typical responses: C—nothing, we have no bootstraps
   B—revolt, take food by force
   A—share equally; defend ourselves; die with everyone else

CLOSING: Bring entire group together. Discuss their feelings and the hunger problem. Expect lots of verbal and non-verbal reactions during and following the game.

118

food experiences that teach

Just as Jesus did (see "Meals Jesus Ate," p. 26), so most of us find that meals and coffee/tea breaks can provide not only nourishment, but also fellowship, conversation, and times of learning.

Mealtimes and snack breaks can also stimulate thinking on the issue of hunger for families and church groups.

The suggestions in this section have been used with many variations around the country. Except for those with sources given, they all have a variety of sources. Several of them are similar. Use them as you find them, or add your own imagination!

(Note: Before you use these experiences, see "Before You Play Any of These Games . . ." on pages 100-101.)

Contents

Number	Game	Setting*
47	Hunger on Spaceship Earth	full meal (luncheon)
48	Coffee Break Game	coffee break
49	Famine—Feast	full meal (dinner)
50	World Distribution Simulation	coffee break
51	Poverty Meals	lunch or dinner
52	Hunger Surprise!	church full meal

*Settings are only suggested. Most games may be adapted for church night suppers, church school class breakfasts, etc.

119

47

Type: Simulation
Time: A Meal or Coffee Break

Hunger on Spaceship Earth

This luncheon-game is meant to provide an experiential framework for understanding some of the inequities of the present socio-economic world situation and some of the feeling of helplessness and frustration that are necessary ingredients of its effects. By enabling the participants to deal with a concrete experience of built-in injustices, it can become a learning tool that goes beyond the merely factual. The aim of the experience should be closely tied up with the concept of global interdependence. How it is resolved in the concrete situation will demonstrate in a very particular way the positive and negative aspects of interdependence, and should bring to the fore both the critical danger involved as well as the potential for hope and well-being.

PLAYERS: The game is best played with at least thirty people, in order to have a more visible proportion of rich and poor. You might use the following figures in proportioning your players and resources.

	Population	Players	Resources	Chips Per Player
First World	6%	2	40%	38
Second World	33%	9	40%	9
Third World	61%	19	20%	2

From *Hunger on Spaceship Earth Simulation Game,* produced by the World Hunger Project, New York Metropolitan Regional Office of the American Friends Service Committee, 15 Rutherford Place, New York, NY 10003. Used by permission.

You will have to make adaptations of these figures if you have more or fewer players, but you can base this on the population distribution.

There should be two persons available for selling food and visas.

SETTING: We have prepared the game around the setting of a luncheon buffet, but this can easily be adapted to a "coffee hour" or "snacktime." Feel free to adapt the menu any way you like; this merely represents one that was used successfully.

The food or buffet table should be made to look as attractive as possible. A beautifully furnished table and chairs should be placed in a removed and comfortable area of the room for the First World players. Provide a modest table and chairs for Second World players. The Third World players should be confined to a small and unfurnished section of the room, providing only chairs or sitting room on the floor. There ought to be a visible difference in the three settings.

MATERIALS: Each player should receive three items: a menu (see samples below), a role-identity instruction sheet, and an envelope of chips corresponding to his/her role identity (see table above).

For thirty players you will need:

First World Role-Identity Sheets   2
     Chips 76

Second World Role-Identity Sheets   9
     Chips 76; ½ Chips 10

Third World Role-Identity Sheets   19
     Chips 2; ½ Chips 72

Visas   14

Extra: ½ Chips – 28

(These extra ½ chip pieces can be used if you have more than thirty players or can be used at the luncheon table for change.)

121

SAMPLE MENUS: (May be duplicated or written out by hand)

YOUR MENU			
Meat or cheese	–	1 slice	– 4 chips
Salad	–	1 portion	– 6 chips
Rolls, bread	–	each	– 3 chips
Butter	–	1 portion	– ½ chip
Pastry	–	1 portion	– 5 chips
tea	–		– 1
coffee	–		– 1
milk	–		– ½
sugar	–		– ½
condiments	–		– ½
rice dish	–	1 portion	– 1 chip
tea	–		– ½
raisins	–	1 portion	– ½
cracker	–	1 portion	– ½

HAVE A HAPPY DAY!

SAMPLE ROLE IDENTITY SHEETS: May be printed on the back of the menus or distributed separately.)

Welcome to the First World . . .

You are a privileged citizen of the First World.

You are one of the 6% of the earth's population who are "developed," and you have almost unlimited enjoyment of the goods of the earth.

You are invited to enjoy the luncheon we have prepared for you. You have been given 38 chips which entitle you and your fellow First World traveler to enjoy at least 40% of all that is being served.

Because you enjoy a high level of well being, health, literacy, and culture, you are granted an unconditional visa to travel anywhere you choose.

Don't forget your camera! Enjoy your day!

122

Welcome to the Second World . . .

You are a member of the "developing" peoples of the world, a citizen of one of the progressing industrialized countries—most likely of the Eastern Soviet Bloc.

You are one of the 33% of the world's people who use and control approximately 40% of the earth's goods. You have been given a relative buying power in your packet of 9 chips. Please feel free to purchase whatever you can from the luncheon table.

Since you enjoy a minimum level of literacy and good health, you are free to travel to the countries of the Third World under these conditions:

1) you must travel in pairs;

2) visas must be purchased at luncheon table. 1 chip must be deposited at luncheon table, ½ chip must be granted to Third World country you visit.

Don't forget your camera! Enjoy your day!

Welcome to the Third World . . .

You are hereby classified as a citizen of the Third World. Unfortunately that will be of some disadvantage to your participation in this luncheon.

Since you comprise 61% of the world's population, it is not quite possible for you to have full freedom in consumption of the earth's resources, or in fact, of our luncheon. You are entitled to about 20% of the earth's goods and have been given a relative buying power of 2 chips. We encourage you to be creative and enterprising in efforts to increase your buying power, perhaps through combining your chips.

Due to your high level of disease and illiteracy, we regret to inform you that your travel permissions are restricted. You must stay in the territory designated *Third World*. No more than 3 persons may be issued visas for outside travel at one time.

Cost: Visa to Second World — 7 chips
        Visa to First World — 9 chips

Don't forget your camera! Enjoy the luncheon!
(Visas may be purchased at luncheon table)

Sample Visa and Chip Sheets (Use colored paper if possible):

you will need 14 visas, 154 chips (value 1) and 110 chips($\frac{1}{2}$)

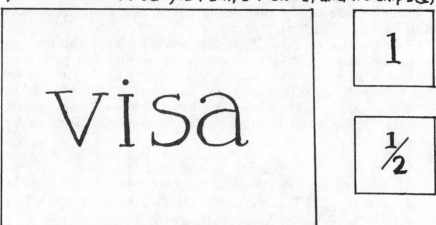

if cut from 9"x12" construction paper visas may be $2\frac{1}{4}$" x $3\frac{1}{4}$"
if cut from $8\frac{1}{2}$"x11"; 2"x3" (see diagram below left)

chips are most easily cut out in rows of eleven (14 rows of value 1, 10 rows of value $\frac{1}{2}$) 3/4" squares will cut from either size paper.

RULES: If you know the players, it would be a good idea to place a strong personality in each of the three "worlds." This could be done as you give each player his/her materials. Should you not know the players, simply give a set of materials to each player at random. If you plan a lecture, or visual presentation, complete that before distributing the materials. It is best for players to "begin cold," without a chance for discussion of their role identities, relative wealth, etc., prior to the start of the game.

124

As verbal directions, you might tell the participants:

a) that this is a simulation game approximating the distribution of purchasing power, population, and food as it is in the real world;

b) that they are to deal with the situation as they see it, and enjoy the meal;

c) that there are no rules other than those on their role-identity sheet.

Designate the person to sell visas and the person to collect payment for food.

The dilemma of how to deal with the inequities of the food distribution may take several forms. It is well to be prepared for them. Example: The group may immediately take on a "just and humane" style, and work toward providing every player with an equal or adequate share of food. This is of course the ideal, and will not necessarily happen.

It might happen that the game results in "confrontation" or "revolution." In that case, it should be resolved by having the sides draw up a statement of "grievance" or "justification," etc. This should express both their feelings and their extended methodology for remedying the situation.

The facilitator should use good judgment to surmise when the game has been played out and call its end. At the finish, it is well to invite the players to drop the rules and share the food. However, you might judge it beneficial to let the inequality go unresolved. This would not be recommended if the session were to continue at any length (i.e., workshop or long discussion).

DEBRIEFING: The debriefing session is very important and should be led by someone able to help uncover people's reactions and synthesize their perceptions and insights. This should provide valuable motivation for further in-depth study of the tremendously complex problems involved in the concrete global situation.

SUGGESTED DEBRIEFING QUESTIONS:

a) What was your emotional reaction to the rules? To the rules of other groups?

b) How did you feel toward the people in the other group?

c) Did you agree with the manner in which your group resolved the problem? Do you think it was realistic?

d) Did your feelings change drastically during the experience? If so, when? Why?

48

Type: Simulation
Time: 15-30 minutes

Coffee Break Game

This probably should *not* be the first item on your agenda. During a hunger study, at an appropriate time suggest that your group take a coffee break, and then use this exercise *without warning the group ahead of time that the break is also a hunger game!*

PREPARATION BEFOREHAND: Make name tags in 3 colors or in 3 shapes. According to the size of your group, use the following ratios:

1 in Group #1	3 in Group #II	6 in Group #III
(First World)	(Second World)	(Third World)

Distribute these tags when participants come into the room, without making any statement about their being different. If anyone asks why they are different, merely say casually you'll tell them later.

PROCEDURE: Announce the coffee break. Tell each person to go to the coffee break area represented by his/her name tag. (You might color code tables, dangle appropriate shapes above them to match name tags, or merely point them out.) Ask them to go to the designated areas and *remain within them* during the entire break.

The First World should have an elaborate area with choices of coffee, tea, cocoa or punch, cream, sugar, lemon, cookies or cake, spoons, and more than enough chairs. You might even use a lace cloth and silver, flowers, etc. to provide a setting of luxury.

The Second World should have an adequate setting, with either coffee or tea, cream and sugar, not quite enough spoons and just enough chairs. Serve them in mugs or paper cups, and use a plain cloth, if any.

126

The Third World (with the most people) should have inadequate supplies. They should have lukewarm water, a few teabags or about three spoonfuls of instant coffee, no cream or sugar, no spoons and only one or two chairs. No tablecloth, of course!

There should be some separation between groups, but they should be visible to one another. Permit them to eat for 5-10 minutes, watching dynamics for later discussion. Then call the group together.

Ask: How did you feel about being where you were? About the other two groups?

Why did you think you were put in the group you were?

What happened—was there sharing? stealing?

You might point out two less obvious parallels between this game and the real world: a) people have no control over the "world" they are assigned to at birth, and (b) each world is fully visible to the other two.

You may, of course, decide to end the break by permitting everyone to have a "real" (i.e. First World) break, or you may ask the group to make that decision.

49

Type: Simulation
Time: Mealtime

Famine — Feast

This is a mealtime version of the Coffee Break Game. It is most appropriate for a church night supper, church luncheon, or workshop meal.

PREPARATION BEFOREHAND: Make name tags in 3 colors or in 3 shapes. According to the size of your group, use the following ratios:

1 in Group I	3 in Group II	6 in Group III
(First World)	(Second World)	(Third World)

Distribute these tags when participants enter the room, without making any statement about their being different. If anyone asks, be as casual as you can, so as not to arouse suspicion.

PROCEDURE: Announce the meal. As persons go through the serving line, servers give them a meal that corresponds to their name tags.

FIRST WORLDERS GET:
Meat	Salad
Rice	Bread and Butter
A Vegetable	Dessert

SECOND WORLDERS GET:
Rice	Salad
A Vegetable	

THIRD WORLDERS GET: A small portion of rice

As they leave the serving line, First Worlders are directed to a table lavishly set with flowers, lace cloth, perhaps silver. Second Worlders are sent to a table with a rough or paper cloth, paper cups, no flowers. Third Worlders are sent to a bare table off in one corner of the room with only a couple of chairs around it.

Observe the group during the meal for dynamics.

When they have been eating for about 5 minutes, stop the game for an announcement. "May I have your attention, please? First Worlders, we just want to tell you that there's a lot of food in the kitchen, and you are entitled to all you want. Please go back for as much as you will. That's all. Thanks." *Be sure* to use the phrase "You are entitled to all you want," because the catch here is that they can get any they want not only for themselves, but for anyone else! But don't say that . . . see if they figure it out.

When the meal is over, it is essential to call the group together to discuss what happened and how members of each world felt. You might use such questions as:

How did you feel when you saw what your name tag meant?

Did you think this game was "fair"? Why or why not?

How did you feel about your world? About those in the other two?

How did our group deal with the situation? What are some other ways we might have dealt with it?

As a member of the real First World, how do you react to this game?

50

Type: Simulation
Time: 1 hour to 1½ hours

World Distribution Simulation

PURPOSE:

To enable people to experience the distribution of three basic components in today's world: space, population, and material goods.

PREPARATION BEFOREHAND:

Use this diagram to set up the room before people arrive:

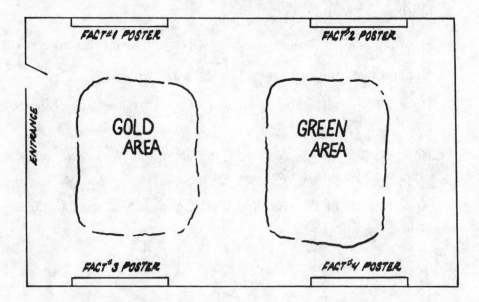

Outline gold and green areas on the floor using crepe paper and masking tape.

Make posters of each of the following four facts and tape them to the walls where indicated.

Taken from A Study/Action Kit: Metamorphosis: Christians Choosing Lifestyles for a World in Crisis (Atlanta: John Knox Press).

130

Fact 1: The two greatest drains on the global environment are widespread population growth in some underdeveloped countries and rising rates of consumption in industrial nations. The global consumptions of goods and services is due about equally to the population explosion and to the rise of individual affluence. (Richard Brown, "Rich Countries and Poor in a Finite, Interdependent World," *Daedalus* [Fall, 1973] p. 153 ff.)

Fact 2: With about 6% of the world's population, the United States uses approximately 35% of the world's raw materials.

Fact 3: Conversion of grain into meat is an inefficient way to get food value. It takes 7 lbs. of grain to produce 1 lb. of beef. Per capita consumption in the U.S.A. has grown from 55 lbs. in 1940 to 117 lbs. in 1972. (Lester Brown, "Global Food Insecurity," *The Futurist,* April, 1974, pp. 56 ff.)

Fact 4:	Population	Land Area
Asia	55%	16%
N. America	6%	15%

—1974 Year Book, *Encyclopedia Britannica*

After estimating how many persons you expect, place ample chairs in the green area. Place one chair in the gold area. (You may also want to make the green area extravagant with soft music, flowers, candelabra, etc.)

Set up a serving table in each area as follows:

a. In gold area provide enough coffee, juice, and donuts for the estimated attendance.

b. In the green area provide cream and sugar for coffee.

PROCEDURE:

As persons enter, place green or gold armbands on them in a ration of 7 gold to 3 green. This simulates the distribution of population according to affluence: the green area represents North America and Europe and the gold area represents the remainder of the world, which is less affluent.

Ask persons to go to the area of their armband color and to stay there without eating or drinking.

After everyone has entered the room, two persons from the *gold* area are asked to take *all* but two cups of coffee, two glasses

131

of juice, and two donuts to the table in the green area. They then return to their gold area.

All are now invited to eat and drink for 10-15 minutes. Participants dine in their own areas. After 5 minutes of the refreshment period, the game assistant asks people in the gold area to send one person from their group to the green area to ask for coffee, donuts and juice.

At this point the game is completely spontaneous. The people in the gold area may choose not to send anyone to the green area. The people in the green area may or may not offer their resources.

After the refreshment period is over, have a "debriefing" session for 30-45 minutes. During this period, make sure that children are not neglected—keep an alert ear for their responses. The debriefing session will focus on two types of questions—subjective and objective.

SUBJECTIVE QUESTIONS:

How did each of you feel during this experience?

How did each group respond to asking for or giving refreshments?

At what points did you feel guilty, compassionate, angry, bitter, arrogant, or happy?

OBJECTIVE QUESTIONS:

Take time for participants to read and think about the four fact posters on the walls, then reflect on the following questions:

Do Christians have a right to consume all they can pay for?

Studies indicate that when standards of living are raised from a mere survival level, population growth rates decline. Can you think of reasons why persons are willing to limit family size as standards of living improve? What implications does this fact have for Christian responsibility in today's world?

Should Americans make an effort to reduce their consumption of beef for the sake of a more efficient use of available grains for the hungry of the world?

132

51

Type: Simulation
Time: Mealtime

Poverty Meals

Persons concerned about hunger have devised several menus and settings for meals which permit participants to actually experience identification with the world's hungry while contributing to hunger relief. The usual procedure is to provide a very simple menu (which has been announced ahead of time) for which a regular price is charged. Partakers understand ahead of time that the difference between the actual cost of their meal and the cost of the regular meal will be sent to a pre-determined hunger cause.

SUGGESTED MENUS:

Brown rice, unsweetened tea

Cooked dried beans, unsweetened tea

Peanut butter sandwich (no jelly), milk (the milk and peanut butter make a complete protein)

Simple soup, cornbread, fruit, beverage

52

Hunger Surprise!

This is the nastiest game in the book, which is why I saved it for last. Anyone planning to play this one, please don't invite me!

This works best with a whole congregation or fairly large group, and especially well immediately after a hunger worship service.

PROCEDURE: Announce that a churchwide meal will be served immediately after worship. During the service, have some persons preparing the food, being sure it's the kind of food that smells delicious . . turkey, ham, roasts, vegetables, pies, breads—anything that *smells*. Be sure these smells are reaching those who plan to attend the meal. About the time participants are going to be coming in, load all the food onto a table in the center of the dining room.

Meanwhile, prepare enough rice for each diner to have one scoopful, and enough tea for each to have one cup (unsweetened). Set dining tables in such a way that the laden table is in full view (and in full smell).

When participants enter, direct them to seats, telling them they will be served. Then serve them—rice and tea. Announce as they are being served that unfortunately no members of the First World were able to attend the meal, only Third Worlders. But the First Worlders' food will be held for them.

Observe dynamics for later discussion. Either in small groups at tables or as a larger group, discuss both how the participants felt about the meal and what happened. You might use such questions as:

How do you feel about being tricked? Might persons in the Third World feel similarly about being born where they were?

Against whom did you feel what you felt? (anger? disappointment, etc.)

Did it matter that everybody also had rice and tea? Or did you feel you really ought to get a First World meal anyway?

How did our group deal with this situation? What did you hear and/or see?

Then ask the $64,000 question: what shall we do with the food? (Note: I have been told it's cheating to eat it!)

appendix

I
Additional Suggestions for Families

Families concerned to make hunger action a daily part of their lives have come up with many effective ways to do so. Among them:

1. *The Unseen Guest:* At each meal, or at one meal a day (week), a place is set for one additional diner. In the opening blessing, Jesus is asked to "Be our guest," and the family remembers his words, "If you did it to the least of my brothers, you did it to me." Therefore, the cost of the meal is calculated and the price of one additional diner is figured, which is placed in a hunger bank and donated to a hunger cause.

2. *Tithe the Grocery Bill:* Some families figure the cost of their own food for a month and give ten percent of that to a hunger cause. Others routinely purchase food each shopping trip equal to roughly one-tenth of their total bill, and donate the food to hunger crisis centers. Still others make one shopping trip in ten specifically for the purpose of buying food to give to a crisis center. In each case, one-tenth of the amount the family eats is returned to the Lord, calling to mind the ancient Israelite custom of tithing the first fruits and animals.

3. *World Hunger Banks:* Some families spend an evening together making hunger banks out of discarded tin cans. The cans are washed, rough edges smoothed, then covered with decorative covers of paper or contact paper. Hunger pictures or Christian symbols may be added. Some families keep their banks on the dining table and regularly deposit money in them. Others put them on their coffee tables and deposit loose change there. Still others let each family member keep his or her bank privately, then combine them when their congregation has a hunger offering.

4. *Catch and Save:* One family who lives near water lets the children regularly fish for dinner, and the market price of the fish they catch for eating is given to fight world hunger.

5. *Third World Evening:* Several families regularly observe one meal a week which is considerably simpler than usual—but still nutritious. The difference between the cost of that meal and the cost of a regular meal is then donated to fight hunger.

136

II
Suggested Additional Resources

Many of the games included in this anthology come from larger kits which combine games, hunger facts, suggestions for action, and theolological statements. Groups interested in really delving into the problem of hunger and in seeking solutions are encouraged to use one of the following:

Hunger on Spaceship Earth — a Simulation Game, by Jerald Ciekot and Sister Miriam-Therese.

Order from: New York Metropolitan Regional Office of the
American Friends Service Committee
15 Rutherford Place
New York, NY 10003 ($1.50 plus 50 cents for
postage and handling)

Guidance Manual: Models and Helps to Organize a CROP Walk for the Hungry, Conduct a CROP Canvass, Promote CROP Fast, Carry Out CROP Work Day.

Order from: National CROP Office
P.O. Box 968
Elkhart, IN 46514

Seeds of Change (and other fun things for kids to do)
A brochure listing audio visuals and other materials for children put out by CROP (address above)

World Hunger Crisis Kit: Hope for the Hungry
Robert Woito, editor. Order from:
World Without War Council Publications Bookstore
67 East Madison, Suite 1417
Chicago, IL 60603

Metamorphosis Study/Action Kit published by John Knox Press

Order from: Materials Distribution Service
341 Ponce de Leon Ave., N.E.
Atlanta, GA 30308

Hunger Activities for Children (packet, filmstrip, kit)

Order from: Brethren House Ministries
6301 56th Avenue North
St. Petersburg, FL 33709

BOOKS YOU MAY FIND HELPFUL:

Basic Information on Hunger, including theology:

Christian Responsibility in a Hungry World by C. Dean Freudenberger & Paul M. Minus, Jr. (Abingdon Press, 1976, paperback).

Who Really Starves? Women and World Hunger by Lisa Leghorn and Mary Roodkowsky (Friendship Press, 1977, paperback).

New Hope for the Hungry by Larry Minear (Friendship Press, 1975, paperback).

What Do You Say to a Hungry World? by Stanley Mooneyham (Word Books, 1975).

Your Need for Bread Is Mine: Resources for Helping the Hungry by Morris D. Pike (Friendship Press, 1977, paperback). Excellent for children and younger teens.

Rich Christians in an Age of Hunger: A Biblical Study by Ronald J. Sider (Inter-Varsity Press, 1977, paperback).

Bread for the World by Arthur Simon (Paulist Press, 1975, paperback).

138

BOOKS HELPFUL IN SIMPLER LIVING:

Alternate Celebrations Catalogue, published by Alternatives, 4274 Oaklawn Drive, Jackson, Miss. 39206. (Also available in bookstores.)

How to Live Better on Less: A Guide for Waste Watchers by Barbara Jurgensen (Augsburg Publishing House, 1974, paperback).

Diet for a Small Planet by Frances Moore Lappé (Ballantine Books, 1975, paperback).

More-with-Less Cookbook: Suggestions by Mennonites on how to eat better and consume less of the world's limited food resources by Doris Janzen Longacre (Herald Press, 1976, paperback).

Small Is Beautiful: Economics as if People Mattered by E.F. Schumacher (Harper & Row, 1973, paperback).

Taking Charge: Personal and Political Change through Simple Living by the Simple Living Collective, American Friends Service Committee, San Francisco (Bantam Books, 1977, paperback).

III

Biblical References Included in Games

Reference*	Games
Genesis 1:29	God Feeds People!, Following Food Through the Bible
Genesis 3:1-13	Following Food Through the Bible
Genesis 3:17-19	Following Food Through the Bible
Genesis 4:1-8	Following Food Through the Bible
Genesis 25:29-34	Following Food Through the Bible
Genesis 41:53–42:7	Following Food Through the Bible
Exodus 3:7-8	God Feeds People!, Following Food Through the Bible
Exodus 12:1-17	Following Food Through the Bible
Exodus 16	God Feeds People!, Following Food Through the Bible
Deuteronomy 8:7-17	Profiting from Prophets
Deuteronomy 15:7-11	Profiting from Prophets, How Much Do you Know?
Ruth 1:1-5; 3; 4:18-22	Following Food Through the Bible
1 Samuel 2:12-17; 3:1-14	Following Food Through the Bible
1 Kings 17:1-16	God Feeds People!, Following Food Through the Bible
Isaiah 55:1-3	Profiting from Prophets, Following Food Through the Bible, How Much Do You Know?
Isaiah 58:5-8	God Feeds People! Profiting from Prophets, How Much Do You Know?
Lamentations 4:3-9	Profiting from Prophets, How Much Do You Know?

*When a reference appears in more than one Gospel, the earliest reference is usually used. Some games use one part of a reference, and other games another part; references are given for entire events or teachings.

140

Reference	Games
Hosea 2:1-13	Following Food Through the Bible
Amos 9:13-15	Profiting from Prophets, How Much Do You Know?
Micah 4:1-4	Profiting from Prophets, Following Food Through the Bible
Matthew 4:1-4	Following Food Through the Bible, Parable Put-ups, He Said It!
Matthew 4:19	Parable Put-ups, Parable Placemats, He Said It!
Matthew 5:13	God Feeds People!, Parable Put-ups, Parable Placemats, He Said It!
Matthew 6:11	Parable Put-ups
Matthew 7:18	Parable Put-ups, Parable Placemats
Matthew 9:10	Meals Jesus Ate
Matthew 12:1-2	Meals Jesus Ate
Matthew 12:33	He Said It!
Matthew 13:3-8	Parable Put-ups
Matthew 13:24-30	Parable Put-ups
Matthew 13:31-32	Parable Put-ups
Matthew 13:33	Parable Put-ups, Parable Placemats, He Said It!
Matthew 13:38	He Said It!
Matthew 13:47-50	Parable Put-ups
Matthew 14:13-21	Meals Jesus Ate
Matthew 15:32-38	Meals Jesus Ate
Matthew 17:20	Parable Put-ups, He Said It!
Matthew 25:31-46	Profiting from Prophets, Parable Put-ups, Scripture Mini-skits, World Geography Lesson, Unto One of the Least of These
Matthew 26:6-7	Meals Jesus Ate
Matthew 26:17-29	Following Food Through the Bible, Meals Jesus Ate
Mark 1:30-31	Meals Jesus Ate

Reference	Games
Mark 6:30-44	God Feeds People!, Following Food Through the Bible
Luke 6:20-25	The Debate, Parable Put-ups, He Said It!
Luke 7:34	Meals Jesus Ate
Luke 7:36	Meals Jesus Ate
Luke 10:38-42	Meals Jesus Ate
Luke 11:37	Meals Jesus Ate
Luke 14:1-24	Meals Jesus Ate
Luke 14:15-24	Parable Put-ups
Luke 15:11-24	Parable Put-ups
Luke 16:19-31	Parable Put-ups, Scripture Mini-skits, Letter from Beyond
Luke 19:1-10	Following Food Through the Bible, Meals Jesus Ate
Luke 24:13-35	God Feeds People!, Following Food Through the Bible, Meals Jesus Ate
Luke 24:42	Meals Jesus Ate
John 2:1-11	Following Food Through the Bible, Meals Jesus Ate
John 4:7-42	Meals Jesus Ate
John 6:3-13	Scripture Mini-Skits
John 6:35	Parable Put-ups, Parable Placemats, He Said It!
John 12:1-3	Meals Jesus Ate
John 15:1-5	Parable Put-ups, Parable Placemats, He Said It!
John 21:4-13	Following Food Through the Bible, Meals Jesus Ate
Acts 2:42	Following Food Through the Bible
Acts 6:1-6	Following Food Through the Bible
Acts 10:1-35	Following Food Through the Bible
1 Corinthians 10:14-24	Following Food Through the Bible
Revelation 19:6-9	God Feeds People!, Following Food Through the Bible